CROSS OVER

Your Greatest You Awaits You

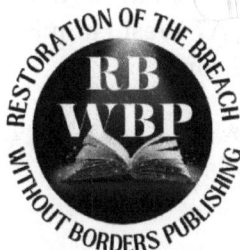

RB WBP
RESTORATION OF THE BREACH
WITHOUT BORDERS PUBLISHING

West Palm Beach, Florida

REV. LEOSTONE MORRISON

For permission requests, please contact:
restorativeauthor@gmail.com

ISBN: 978-1-954755-05-5

Published and formatted by:
Restoration of the Breach without Borders
133 45th Street, Building A7 West Palm Beach, Florida 33407
restorativeauthor@gmail.com
Tele: (475) 233-9008

EBook Cover Design by:
Leostone Morrison

Editing done by:
Bishop Omar Wedderburn
omardiweddaman@gmail.com

Melisha Bartley-Ankle
melbarxtd@yahoo.com

Juan Pablo
Juanpablo_20@hotmail.com

Unless otherwise stated Scripture verses are quoted from the New King James Version of the Bible.

Dedication

This book is dedicated to everyone who knows God has prepared more for them than they are presently living and are willing to pursue living and serving God at a higher dimension. Cross Over into your best you.

Acknowledgments

To the Holy Spirit, my Primary Destiny Helper. I am elated to know that my assignment was not completed with the fifth book- Marriage Reconstruction. I am blessed with the family I have. Sherene, my wife; your support has increased as the assignments from the Lord increase. You continue to prove that you are truly my gift from God.

Hillary Dunkley Campbell, you have come into my life for such a time as this. Your kind words of endorsements are appreciated and your continued support with the assignments of Restoration of the Breach Without Borders Ministry. I thank you unsparingly.

To KristoJay Paul, you unreservedly read the raw manuscript and gave your truthful endorsement. I thank you immensely. I pray that your ministry will continue to expand as you sing and to the glory of God.

My colleague and friend Bishop Wedderburn, I thank you for writing such a beautiful foreword. Being the author of two powerful books, you know the necessity of an honest foreword. I pray you will continue to make yourself available to the Kingdom of God. I look forward to continued partnership.

Introduction

The journey continues! In the book, *Mind Renewal: Biblical Secrets to A Better You*, Rev Leostone Morrison explicitly said, "Mind renewal is not an event but a journey". This book, Cross Over, is a continuation of your mind's transformational journey. Cross Over covers several topics that, if mastered, will produce a significant impact not only for yourself, but generations to come. This book is not intended for information only, but rather, for the application of the received information. James exhorts us in his letter to be doers of the word and not just hearers (James 1:22). You must graduate from the hearing to the doing class. Cross Over promises, if applied, to be life-changing. May the Holy Spirit guide you as you read and apply it to your life.

Endorsements

Crossing Over to your "Next" or to "Your Better You" may come with life challenges. Rev. Leostone Morrison in his latest masterpiece has done an excellent job in giving us the tools and strategies to help us to do so effectively and successfully. "Seeing the wealth in your pain", "Disappointed into your appointment", and "Too Much to Gain to Lose" are some of the topics that he so eloquently writes about to engage you into a deeper understanding of what it truly means to Cross Over. This I must say is indeed the prequel to the best-seller "Mind Renewal: Biblical Keys to a Better You".

-Hillary Dunkley Campbell
Author
I Am Encouraged; Jesus Saves; What Is
Stopping You

*****

Cross Over is a book for anyone desirous of a richer, fuller relationship with the Almighty God. In these end times, radical changes are necessary to be a true warrior for Jesus Christ. Cross Over touches the deep recesses of the heart and mind for individuals to see who they are versus who they should be in His image - of great worth and precious in His sight. It is relevant for this season, equipping us to be stronger for what is ahead. Cross Over into this knowledge and revelation and be blessed and empowered in Jesus Christ.

-Kristojay Paul
Gospel Artist
Gospel Radio Announcer

Foreword

Rev. Leostone Morrison, fellow author and colleague in the Kingdom, did a tremendous job on this book. *Cross Over* is a stunning continuation of Mind Renewal, a phenomenal work previously done by him.

Rev. Morrison offers his readers transformative keys for crossing over to a renewed life. Albeit the peril that lies ahead on the traversing path, Rev. Morrison was not short in delivering insightful and valuable knowledge for the sojourners exploring the pages of his book to unlock their full potential as designed by the Lord.

Yet, even with that said, when faced with the storm of life, many quickly forget the Lord's promises and power to preserve and protect them from it. Rev. Morrison enlightens his readers about the Lord's inability to lie or fail. Therefore, they must not be distracted while in transit.

One time ago, the disciples were guilty of making such a mistake. Jesus had just concluded teaching a large gathering of people by the seaside and having dismissed the multitude, He entered a ship and instructed (an imperative command) His disciples to "go over on the other side." However, while on their way to the other side, there rose a great storm and the disciples were fearful. Immediately they had forgotten Jesus' instruction to cross over when fear set in. They were distracted by the sea surge that broke onto the ship, as the waves going into the vessel were greater than the water they could bail out.

As humans it is worrying having to deal with external problems and having those extremities come crashing in like waves, now that's a different experience entirely. Rev. Morrison takes his readers on a journey of such realities - the craziness of life's problems crashing in all at once! He brings awareness of the accuser's mind games during these ordeals that have the believers questioning their faith, just as the disciples did in thinking they were going to die.

Another key worth noting is that Jesus was asleep in the ship's stern. Have you ever felt like God is asleep on you; when you need Him the most He is not around? The disciples questioned Jesus, "Don't you care if we perish? "Jesus responded in rebuking their fear. After all, He is onboard, it will not sink! So here is another vital cross-over key, do not allow storms to wreck your minds - sleep through them and be at peace!

Satan utilizes fear against the Christian community - one of his many devices employed to deter them from God's promises. Rev. Morrison advises Christians to not be preoccupied with what is opposing them as doing so will cause loss of sight and sound mind. He articulates, "Where fear is present, faith is absent."

The Hebrew writer says, "Without faith, it is impossible to please God." (Hebrews 11:6) The Greek meaning for impassible translates as impotent, without strength, weakly. Powerless, disabled, unable to be done. Therefore, fear (the absence of faith) renders one powerless before God.

Not to worry, *Cross Over* offers a plethora of tools of faith in getting over on the other side, even the kind that allows you to walk on water. Readers are encouraged to keep faith amidst horrid storms - survival does not exclude the harsh experiences but how they are handled will determine success. One can either cower in fear or trust God that He is more than able to bring you through.

Cross Over is a book for the season, a reliable tool to have in your possession, a guide during troublesome times, and a daily devotional jam-packed with divine knowledge and wisdom. Are you ready to Cross Over?

-Bishop O'mar Wedderburn.
Author, Speaker, Counselor

TABLE OF CONTENTS

CHAPTER ONE
NOTHING SHALL BE WASTED/
PAIN

Pain is no respecter of person or time; it does not check to see if you are ready or if it is invited. Pain is not like the Holy Spirit who is a gentle being and desires to be invited in. It is a bully. Not just a bully but a dictator. Pain desires to control your thoughts, actions, and in general your entire life. Pains' ultimate goal is not to nullify you in every facet of your life but to reposition you. Where you are shifted to, depends not on pain but upon you.

The truth is none of us are exempted from pain. Therefore, before you judge or crucify your next intended victim, please consider this question; can you walk a mile in the person's shoes? Not a day, only a mile. Can you handle the pain of their struggle and their responsibilities that have become overbearing? Please be encouraged today; never allow the battering of others to crush you; instead, excavate the wealth of your pain.

PAIN DEPOSITS

The bank offers several services, such as checking accounts, savings accounts, certificates of deposit, and loans, including car loans and home mortgages. Further services may include safe deposit boxes and investment-related services. When you look at a bank slip, you see deposits and withdrawals. There can be no withdrawals if there are no deposits, it is impossible; nothing in, nothing out.

Every pain, hurt, or disappointment that has graced your shores are deposits made into your possibility account. They function like seeds in the ground. As time passes, your pain deposits come to maturity and withdrawal becomes available. It was Jesus who told the parable of the wheat and the tares growing together until the day of harvest (Mathew 13:24-30). The truth is each pain deposit is embedded in its duality in the harvest. You must decide what you withdraw. Where there is poverty there is also wealth.

The hurt that one experiences comes not in finality but with choices. You can choose to become poorer or richer by the sad events. Was it a sad event only or was it a seed of wealth and prosperity parading in the fabrics of sadness? Truth is, that depends on how you perceive and respond. If people knew the wealth, they were giving you when they hurt and rejected you, they would not have. You are wealthier today because of the hurt that was levied on you. The hurt sits as a goldmine waiting to be discovered. People are living in lack or insufficiency because they have failed to excavate the gold from their hurt. You were handpicked for the hurt you received, but more than the hurt, the wealth. The more pain you have been entrusted with; the more wealth is required of you. The scripture exhorts us in this wise, *'to whomsoever much is given, of him shall be much required: and to whom men have committed much, of him they will ask the more.'* Luke 12:48b.

How you respond to the hurt determines how the wealth responds to you. You can choose to miss the wealth by focusing on the hurt. You need to maximize or reap the benefits of the hurt that was bestowed upon you. The hurt was compared to a goldmine. Gold must be excavated, meaning, you will have to dig deep. Refuse to merely scrape at the shoreline through the rubble (lies, cheating, abuse, and other turmoil) of the manifested. Rather, pursue deep wealth diving as you crave the benefits of each hurt. Wealth comes through making use of your pain to produce books, movies, etc.

As you crossover from your present level thinking please embrace this truth, nothing shall be wasted; not the tears, the pain, the hurt, or the abuse shall be wasted. You have ignorantly thrown out your blessings in the dumpster because of the worms and stenches associated with them. The awful odour serves as a deterrent to the needed excavation. This truth is evident in the book of John chapter 11, where Jesus received a message that His friend Lazarus was sick. When He arrived at his house, Martha, Lazarus' sister, said "he is dead." Jesus asked to be taken to where he was laid and she replied, "By now he stinks." One of the most notable miracles Jesus performed resided behind a stinking odor. Jesus then asked for the stone that closed the door to be removed; removal means scent exposure. This is true, many victories have been forfeited because we failed to confront the rotten stench of the situation. Jesus had to be prepared to deal with the odor before he performed the miracle. You are a bad odor away from your miracle.

There are all manners of pain; emotional, spiritual, financial, and physical. However, those are some of the obvious depictions of pain. Please let us equip ourselves today with some of the not-so-obvious.

PAIN IS A MESSENGER

When the body needs repairing, one medium used to inform the owner is through the messenger of pain. Depending on the magnitude of the message from pain, the corresponding necessary urgency must be applied. Recently a colleague received information from the messenger which is painful but underestimated or undervalued what was conveyed. The urgency needed was not activated and death happened swiftly. The person died leaving family members questioning what happened. This is the challenge we face with this messenger. Misreading or misunderstanding the message delivered can become fatal.

Let us create a scenario and use it for our benefit.

> Mary, a Christian girl who was going through a depressing period, had intercourse with John and got pregnant. John said it was not his because they only went together once. She was in the choir, they rejected her followed by the church stripping her of all her responsibilities. Her phone no longer rang. Then she heard that John was getting married to Susan, a member of the choir. Mary felt the pain!
>
> What was the lesson Mary received from the messenger called Pain?
>
> Pain told her, the best way is God's way.
>
> Pain told her, consent to intimacy does not guarantee receiving a wedding ring.
>
> Pain taught her not to be naive - John's profession of love for her did not equate to them having a life together or that he saw her as a wife.
>
> Pain told her, settling for good at the expense of God's best is robbery to self.
>
> Pain taught her that expectations do get shattered. Please read that again.

Pain taught her that there are consequences to walking out of the will of God.

Pain informed her that she would be a single mother.

Pain told her, that the other single females in the church also desired to be married.

You might have noticed that I shifted from "pain told her" To saying, "pain taught her." That is because pain is a teacher. There are certain lessons that you will learn, and pain is the master trainer.

Pain taught her, that those who she was there for might not be there when she needed them most.

Some of you have been taught this same lesson, we sat at the front of the class while some are still in this class. Please pay attention to what pain has and is teaching you; do not miss the lesson.

Pain is a re-router. Please let that sink in.

If all we see is Mary's hurt from John denying her pregnancy and not marrying her, we miss the re-routing component of pain. Pain might just have been the reroute of more devastating hurt. Many people who were rejoicing years ago, had they been rerouted their story would be different today.

So, pain taught her that inequality and unfairness come from even the church.

Another thing we miss about pain is, it is committed. Pain is not one to abandon a relationship. Pain believes in commitment. To cancel a committed relationship with pain, one must become radical, it will not simply get up and leave. Pain will stay with you even when you kick it through the door. Pain is adamant - no divorce, no separation. Some marriages have lasted 6 months, some a year; however, the pain will stay with you until you die, it believes in until death do us part and when you die, it gets involved with your spouse or your children. Pain believes in family.

PAIN IS AN ELEVATOR/STAIRS

An elevator or stairs travels in both directions- up and down. Where pain takes you is not dependent upon pain but upon you, you select the direction. You can choose to be elevated or spiraled downwards because of the unfortunate or fortunate dictates of pain. Being rejected can take you down to a level where you don't realize it because pain can make you numb - you can't feel it, so you don't care.

Pain tells a lot. If it keeps coming back, it means that there are unresolved issues.

PAIN IS AN OPPORTUNITY HIDDEN

Many businesses that are doing well today are the product of pain. Many business ventures start because someone got fired, was redundant, or was seeking employment, found none, and decided to launch out as an entrepreneur. One of the largest seating churches in Jamaica today came out of a painful church situation.

What are the opportunities you have missed that pain provided?

Michelle Jones went through the pain of cancer. She decided to capitalize on that opportunity, and she wrote the book "Cancer on Purpose".

PAIN IS A DIVIDER

Pain separates you from persons who are not in pain. Have you ever heard the saying, 'Misery likes company?' Hurting people are attracted to hurting people.

Perpetual hurt has the strength to rip away the personal values one holds of self. To have that violently taken away has the potential to cause one to lose all self-worth and future thinking. However, that is your choice to make - you can either choose to learn from the hurt or remain broken. The individual can choose to reside at the intended place of demise or enter relaunch mode. This mode is where rediscovering your identity will be found.

RELAUNCH

As hurtful as re-launching can be, it is more painful to wallow in the abyss of failure. According to the Merriam-Webster's Dictionary, relaunch is defined as; *"to launch (something) again or to be launched again, to go into or put (something) into operation or motion again, restarting something."*

It's never too late to start over. We all have had setbacks/failures in our lives. Sometimes defeat seems to get the best of us, and we get overwhelmed. The psychological and financial crowd associated with defeat prevents you from acknowledging that defeat might just be your best friend in hiding. Your best friend refuses to allow you to be successful at the level of your desire because your desire is not a true representation of your availability. A person has indeed failed when maximization of failure is not pursued. What are the gifts that failure blessed you with? But what do you do when faced with a setback? You RELAUNCH, start over. In the book of St Luke, we see a powerful account of re-launching.

One day as Jesus was standing by the Lake of Gennesaret, the people were crowding around him and listening to the word of God. He saw at the water's edge two boats, left there by the fishermen, who were washing their nets. He got into one of the boats, the one belonging to Simon, and asked him to put out a little from shore. Then he sat down and taught the people from the boat. When he had finished speaking, he said to Simon, "Put out into deep water, and let down the nets for a catch." Simon answered, "Master, we've worked hard all night and haven't caught anything. But because you say so, I will let down the net" When they had done so, they caught such a large number of fish that their net began to break. So, they signaled their partners in the other boat to come and help them, and they came and filled both boats so full that they began to sink. When Simon Peter saw this, he fell at Jesus' knees and said, "Go away from me, Lord; I am a sinful man!" For him and all his companions were astonished at the catch of fish they had taken. (Luke 5:1-9)

We see from the above passage men who went out to fish all night and caught nothing. But Jesus told Simon to "Put out into deep water and let down the nets for a catch." Simon said Lord it's useless, we have been at it all night and caught nothing, but we will do as you say. So, in obedience, Simon did as the Lord told him and caught a large number of fish till the nets began to break and they had to call their fellow men to come and help them. Failure here was golden. It was used to position Simon where he could be a blessing to Jesus' Ministry and receive divine life-changing instructions from the Master. Simon relaunched, started over, and was successful.

The disciples were professional fishermen, they knew their trade. They did the best that human knowledge permitted them to do, and it availed nothing. They accepted it, that's how life is. Sometimes you win, sometimes you lose. As you cross over, God is about to overturn some decisions of settling that you have surrendered to. You decided it was over, not worth fighting anymore; but God is not finished. There are persons here reading who God is sending back to where you first had no favorable response. The memories of failure and defeat are not distant, they are very near.

It's where you hear, do it again. Do it again. I know you lost a lot the last time, but this is your winning season. Unfortunately, the belief that success is embedded in the upgrade of the physical provisions continues to diminish the truth of what is available. The disciples used the same boats they previously had no success in and experienced record victories they never thought of. This season is so blessed, you will win where you previously failed.

Every orchestrated failure is overturned right now in the name of Jesus. It took resources to go out to fish. Please commence intentional declarations- in this season; you shall not lose any resources. Everything that pertains to you will yield favorable returns. It is challenging but it is your pulling season. God

11

refuses to let you settle for average, regular, or routine. He is pulling the best out of you. And that might require you to do it again – *RELAUNCHING.*

In this winning season, God is pulling you from logic, ideals, and intellect. He is pulling you to complete trust and obedience in Him. It makes no sense what God is asking you to do but do it. Do not try to understand, reason it out, or explain it. Just do it. This is Him pulling you to a new Dimension. Anything new comes with a lack of knowledge. God will give you new experiences. This is where you have no reference point. You are learning new things about God, trust his pulling and reap.

We see trust, obedience, and success demonstrated in the account of Matthew 17:24-27. *"And when they were come to Peter, and said, Doth not your master pay tribute? He saith, yes. And when he was come into the house, Jesus prevented him, saying, what thinkest thou, Simon? Of whom do the kings of the earth take custom or tribute? Of their own children, or of strangers? Peter saith unto him, of strangers. Jesus saith unto him, 'Then are the children free. Notwithstanding, lest we should offend them, go thou to the sea, and cast an hook, and take up the fish that first cometh up; and when thou hast opened his mouth, thou shalt find a piece of money: that take, and give unto them for me and thee".*

In this pulling, re-launching, winning season, let me haste to tell you: #1. The provisions have already been made; #2. The location is not the place of ordinary; #3. It will be outside of your expectations.

#1. *The provisions have already been made:* It is of great value that you cross over to this truth- God is not perturbed by your echoes of needs. He has not gone into panic mode and is scrambling about seeking to find the answers to your cries. You cross over into new thinking and understanding that the provisions have already been made. Before you came into knowledge of your needs, God knew.

You are being pulled from your regular mode of thinking and expectations. As you relaunch, pass the past, and embrace new beginnings. Embrace what God is doing even if in tight spaces. Do not just trust your intellect or education, they may demote destiny. Have faith in God; you will never receive the extraordinary from the bed of ordinary. Extraordinary withdrawals require extraordinary deposits. Please declare favorable returns and recovery in this season!

There are things that you have attempted and failed, but do not be afraid to cast your net another time. Relaunch, start over, redo whatever needs to be done but do not give up.

God is going to bless you abundantly in the very area where you once collapsed, even your enemies will know that it is the Lord blessing you. Not only that, but you will also be so blessed that your nets will burst, and you will have to call your brothers and sisters to help you. In other words, your receivables will exceed your expectations of preparedness. If at first you fail, try, and try again.

There are times in your life's journey you are faced with something a complicated situation where you are crippled and prevented from acting. You feel weighed down you just want to give up. You are bombarded with crises, one after another, to the point that you are worn down; but relaunch/start over.

The enemy pulls out every trick he has in his book to try and break you because he knows you are a threat to him and his kingdom. Therefore, he uses all he can to get you to give up, but God holds the restart button, which is critical to know. God has the restart button. Partner with God. Get that button activated.

Then you are faced with issues of the heart such as sin, uncontrolled anger, bitterness, and unforgiveness. These are like viruses that affect the heart. In the same manner, a computer is affected by viruses, your heart holds these viruses and they become real problems. They seem to shut you down and destroy your ability to live a life pleasing to God. You need to let go of the junk in your lives that competes against Jesus for our time and attention. So, what do you do when this happens? We relaunch, start over, redo. We ask the Lord for forgiveness, let God push the restart button.

When a computer has viruses, there are sometimes warning signs such as slow performance, difficulty getting rid of pop-up messages that appear out of nowhere, and you can hear the hard drive in constant action, etc. To get rid of the viruses one might do a scan of the hard drive to detect the viruses and then remove them. So, it is with the Holy Spirit and us. When we become infected with viruses, hatred, bitterness, uncontrolled anger, etc., when we hold these viruses in our hearts, we become sick and unhappy, and then we become distracted by the cares of this world and are drawn away from God. But the Holy Spirit, if we let him, scans our hearts, and rids us of those viruses. Look at what the word says in Lamentations 3:22: *"The steadfast love of the LORD never ceases; his mercies never come to an end; they are new every morning; great is your faithfulness."*

An incident happened in my marriage that carried the weight enough to cause a divorce. During the fierce verbal exchange that ensued, my spirit caved to the situation that was raging around me. It seemed like I would not achieve anything, but the Holy Spirit gave me a restart button! He instructed me to activate the restart button of Praise and Worship. The worship re-created the atmosphere which resulted in me being able to focus and prepare for victory. The Lord always provides a way out! The Bible tells us in 1 Corinthians 10:13:

"There hath no temptation taken you but such as is common to man: but God is faithful, who will not suffer you to be tempted above that ye are able; but will with the temptation also make a way to escape, that ye may be able to bear it."

Whenever your heart gets corroded with sin, the restart button of forgiveness is free and is available in abundance.

Forgiveness from God is like welcoming home the prodigal child. We all know the story of the prodigal son, and how his father forgave him when he returned home. His father was overjoyed to have his son back. See Luke 15:11-32. So, it is with our Heavenly Father. He rejoices when we rid ourselves of viruses and come back to him. We must remember that no matter what, our Heavenly Father holds the restart button.

A powerful exhortation comes to you from the book of Job 11:13 which says, *"If thou prepare thine heart and stretch out thine hands toward him; if iniquity be in thine hand, put it far away, and let not wickedness dwell in thy tabernacles."*

Never be afraid to put away anything that is not of God and relaunch. Your mental peace can easily be disturbed and must be protected at all costs. When peace protection is intercepted, your proper thought processing becomes hijacked. Those hijacked thoughts spring into words and those words turn into actions. These actions plummet you into unwelcome defeats. However, no matter what you go through, the situations, the trials, God is there waiting for you with arms wide open, waiting to receive and forgive you. He is saying come home, my child. I am the God of the restart button. Look at the promise of Isaiah 43:18-19 NKJV, *"Do not remember the former things, nor consider the things of old. Behold, I will do a new thing, now it shall spring forth; shall you not know it? I will even make a road in the wilderness and rivers in the desert."*

That position is substantiated by the words of Acts 3: 19-20 which reads: *"Repent therefore and be converted, that your sins may be blotted out, so that times of refreshing may come from the presence of the Lord, and that He may send Jesus Christ, who was preached to you before"*.

When you feel like giving up, when you are faced with uncertainties, remember to relaunch. Throw out your net one more time. Your choices are either give up or relaunch. A part of re-launching is rebranding. Rebranding yourself from the

17

foundations of who you are. Ask yourself, "What do I stand for – what are your core values? Never relinquish your core values unless you have come into greater knowledge, which now exposes them as unhealthy. As you rebrand yourself, the possibilities of discoveries are not illusions. If rediscovering yourself stops at getting you back to where you were, then hurt would have won.

The ripping would have only served as a delay strategy. But if you rediscover and then advance, then your hurt fulfills its purpose of launching you into a higher dimension.

CROSS OVER KEYS

1. Pain is no respecter of person or time. Pain does not check to see if you are ready or if it is invited.
2. Please be encouraged today; never allow the battering of others to crush you. Instead, excavate the wealth of your pain.
3. Every pain, hurt, or disappointment that has graced your shores are deposits made into your possibility account. They function like seeds in the ground.
4. Where there is poverty, there is also wealth.
5. The hurt that one experiences comes not in finality but with choices. You can choose to become poorer or richer by the sad events.

6. You are wealthier today because of the hurt that was levied on you.

7. The more pain you have been entrusted with; the more wealth is required of you.

8. Nothing shall be wasted. Not the tears, the pain, the hurt nor the abuse shall be wasted.

9. Removal means scent exposure. This is true, many victories have been forfeited because you failed to confront the rotten stench of the situation.

10. You are a bad odor away from your miracle.

11. There are certain lessons that you will learn, and pain is the master trainer.

12. Pain is a re-router.

13. Pain believes in commitment. Pain is adamant - no divorce, no separation.

14. Where pain takes you is not dependent upon pain but upon you. You select the direction.

15. A person has indeed failed when maximization of failure is not pursued.

16. Have faith in God; you will never receive the extraordinary from the bed of ordinary. Extraordinary withdrawals require extraordinary deposits.

17. As the heart gets corroded with sin, the restart button of forgiveness is free and is available in abundance.

18. Never be afraid to put away anything that is not of God and relaunch.

19. When you feel like giving up, when you are faced with uncertainties, remember, to relaunch, and throw out your net one more time. The choice is, to give up or relaunch.

20. Never relinquish your core values unless you have come into greater knowledge which now exposes them as unhealthy.

CHAPTER TWO
IT'S AVAILABLE

As a young Christian, I was exposed to miracles, signs, and wonders. I have seen blind eyes opened, the crippled walk, dumb speak, and demon-possessed delivered. I have heard demons speak through persons, and in the name of Jesus, they were cast out. I saw a young lady with an elderly feature receive prayer and her youthful appearance returned. I have seen persons with all manner of illnesses healed, including HIV/AIDS. I have seen miraculous provisions for families and individuals.

These miracles prompted me to ask God for three things: **#1-uncommon favour, #2-uncommon anointing #3-uncommon blessing.** I prayed these requests almost daily until one day the Lord answered me. He said, "Serve me uncommonly." In other words, what you are asking is available, but the dimension of your receiving is directly proportional to the degree of your serving. God's response was that which you have desired is not beyond my capability. It is available. Today please cross over into this truth, it is available! We see a conversation between a Mentor and a Mentee in 2 Kings 2:9-10: *"And it came to pass, when they were gone over, that Elijah said unto Elisha, "Ask what I shall do for thee before I be taken away from thee. And Elisha said, I* *pray thee, let a double portion of thy spirit be upon me. And he said, "Thou hast asked a hard thing: nevertheless, if thou see me when I am taken from thee, it shall be so unto thee; but if not, it shall not be so."*

Please note, Elijah said, the thing you ask for is a hard request, nevertheless... It is available.

I sincerely believe that there are people here who are in their 'nevertheless' season. It's like you are disqualified - worse off than someone who is not next in line. You do not qualify because of your past, your family lineage, the divorce, abortions, prison, etc... Then God says, nevertheless – do not get it twisted. Availability has become possible unto you, not because you earned it, but because of the nevertheless grace of God upon your life. This is the blatant nevertheless favour of God upon you.

I love Elisha's desire. He saw his mentor do great miracles, but he was not satisfied with being a replica, he wanted more. He asked for what he wanted. What do you want from God? Permit me to reiterate, it is available. You have more available to you than you know. Stretch your imagination and stretch it beyond the confines of your normal expectations. Hear this truth, you have not asked because you don't know or believe that it is available.

Nevertheless means "in spite of." So, despite what I have done, in spite of what I think about myself... I can ask God for anything if it is not contrary to his word- knowing that it is available. God is faithful and you can trust the faithfulness of God. However, you must be cognizant of this truth- God is first faithful to Himself.

God will never go against His Word. You must stop limiting what God can supply to you. Stop limiting the dimensions in which God can use you. Recently during a conversation, I expressed how amazing, gifted, and anointed two people I know were. My expression was not from a place of celebration but rather a low dimension of unhealthy comparison. I concluded I was not in their league. As I pondered on what I said, the Holy Spirit said to me, If I can use a donkey, I can use anyone including you. (See Numbers 22:28). Nevertheless... in spite of! Please cross over into this wealth, never judge yourself based on the progress of others, but on your submission to God.

Your true wealth is not measured on the economic scale of the world but upon the level of your obedience to God.

BLATANT FAVOR OF GOD

There are two keywords we will look at, blatant and favour. The definition of blatant according to Merriam-Webster dictionary is a completely obvious, brazen blatant disregard for the rules.

Favour: an act of kindness beyond what is due or usual.

God's unusual kindness towards you is a blatant disregard for the world's expectations of the deserving and undeserving.

This is the season you are in now; this level of favour is beyond what you are deserving. This is where you are overjoyed because you know, by your merit; you do not deserve what is being given to you. In Luke 15:18- 24, we read:

"I will arise and go to my father, and will say unto him, Father, I have sinned against heaven, and before thee, and am no more worthy to be called thy son: make me as one of thy hired servants. And he arose and came to his father. But when he was yet a great way off, his father saw him, and had compassion, and ran, and fell on his neck, and kissed him. And the son said unto him, Father, I have sinned against heaven, and in thy sight, and am no more worthy to be called thy son. But the father said to his servants, 'Bring forth the best robe and put it on him; and put a ring on his hand, and shoes on his feet: And bring hither the fatted calf, and kill it; and let us eat, and be merry: For this my son was dead, and is alive again; he was lost, and is found.' And they began to be merry."

---

1. https://www.merriam-webster.com/dictionary/blatant

2. https://www.encyclopedia.com/humanities/dictionaries-thesauruses-pictures-and-press-releases/favor-0

The Prodigal son dishonored his father and requested his inheritance before his father died. It was like he said, you are taking too long to die, give me my portion now. The father granted him his desire and he left to explore the world. Here is a powerful crossover; please pause to thank God for the blatant favour he bestowed upon you when He did not grant you certain of the desires of your heart. It is true, it was a blatant favour.

Can you imagine if God had approved every desire you possessed? Then Sally's pain (husband) would be yours. The downsizing of the company would have affected you (thank God you did not get that job). The young man wasted all his inheritance and then came to himself. He reasoned the shame I have brought to my father, I am not worthy to return as a son but as a servant. He acknowledged his wrongs and knew it came with consequences. I believe he was a fair young man. Today we see people parading as though their errors do not carry any consequences.

He returned home and spoke the words he rehearsed to say to his father. But pay attention to the father's response. This was highlighted to me by Pastor Jamal Bryant. The father never responded to his son's saying, he ignored him and spoke to the servants. He said starting in vs 22, *'Bring forth the best robe, and put it on him, and put a ring on his hand and shoes on his feet.... for this my son was lost and is found.'* Lord, we thank You for Your blatant favour as expressed in You ignoring us and doing Your will. When the Lord ignores your folly, you should rejoice. The Father's actions declared; that you have suffered the consequences of your errors already. Now it is time to blatantly favour you. Be cognizant of this truth; the blatant favour of God upon you will not always be welcomed by those who judge you unworthy of such honour. We see this demonstrated in Luke 15:25-28: *"Now his elder son was in the field: and as he came and drew nigh to the house, he heard music and dancing. And he called one of the servants and asked what these things meant. And he said unto him, 'Thy brother is come; and thy father hath killed the fatted calf, because he hath received him safe and sound.' And he was angry, and would not go in: therefore, came his father out, and entreated him."*

Please try and understand the venom being unleashed against you from persons are not necessarily against you, but against the blatant favour of God towards you. If the wayward son had returned and accepted as a servant, the older brother would not be wrath. But the blatant favour and great honour of restoration was the source of the older brother's pain. It's true, while you rejoice in the favour of God, others are crippled with pain because of your honour. The old saying goes, "What is a joke to you is death to me". In other words, the effect upon you is not necessarily the same for your peers.

Many persons have plummeted into undue pain because of the blatant favour of God upon their life. Some even encounter sleepless nights. Look at the older son. After a hard day's work, he came home but found no rest. He was tired but stayed outside. Embrace this cross-over truth and understand that when the blatant favour of God is upon you, a big space (where you are) becomes small for your naysayers. Simply because you are there, they begin to suffocate. See Luke 15:29-30: *"And he answering said to his father, 'Lo, these many years do I serve thee, neither transgressed I at any time thy commandment: and yet thou never gavest me a kid, that I might make merry with my friends: But as soon as this thy son was come, which hath devoured thy living with harlots, thou hast killed for him the fatted calf."*

When the older son learned of the blatant favour he spoke in three wise. #1. His goodness and faithfulness. #2. The younger brother's past (wasteful and riotous living). #3. The honour bestowed upon his brother. Please pay attention to this cross-over truth; as the Lord blatantly favour you, the reasons why such honour belongs to someone else will be presented and your past will be exhumed and used against you. You must be at peace with this truth – "That is my past. I am not proud of where I was or have done but to God be the glory, I do not reside there anymore." Your address has been changed. Reject the desires of others to have you bound by the errors of your past. God has forgiven you-you are forgiven.

Do not miss this truth, because of the honour bestowed upon you by God, some have accused Him of being unfair. But I like what TD Jakes said, 'favour ain't fair'. Anyone who has an issue with your received blatant favour, let him/her take it up with God. You did not favour yourself; you did not even earn it; it is a gift from heaven. Hear this; stop trying to justify or explain the favour of God upon your life. Just rejoice and give God all the glory. This is your season of blatant favour from God.

CROSS OVER KEYS

1. The dimension of your receiving is directly proportional to the degree of your serving.
2. Some availabilities have become possible unto you, not because you earned them but because of the nevertheless grace of God upon your life.
3. Stretch your imagination, stretch it beyond the confines of your normal expectations.
4. Hear this truth, you have not asked because you don't know or believe that it's available.

5. You must stop limiting what God can supply to you. Stop limiting the dimensions in which God can use you.

6. Never judge yourself based on the progress of others but on your submission to God.

7. Your true wealth is not measured on the economic scale of the world but upon the level of your obedience to God.

8. God's unusual kindness towards you is a blatant disregard for the rules.

9. Please pause to thank God for the blatant favour he bestowed upon you when He did not grant you certain of the desires of your heart.

10. When the Lord ignores your folly, you should rejoice.

11. Be cognizant of this truth; the blatant favour of God upon you will not always be welcomed by those who judge you unworthy of such honour.

12. Understand that when the blatant favour of God is upon you, a big space (where you are) becomes small for your haters. Simply because you're there, they begin to suffocate.

13. Reject the desires of others to have you bound by the errors of your past. God has forgiven you-you are forgiven.

CHAPTER THREE
LANGUAGES

According to the Oxford Dictionary language is defined as "the method of human communication, either spoken or written, consisting of the use of words in a structured and conventional way." There are 196 countries in the world, and according to an article on Ethnologue.com (last updated on January 1st, 2020, at the time of writing), there are currently seven thousand, one hundred, seventeen (7,117) languages spoken around the world.

Outside of the earthly established languages, there are mediums of communication that are powerful but will not be found in the pages of a dictionary. There are many languages that we are unaware of or have not mastered. Languages that are not defined with characters, symbols, etc. such as English, Spanish, etc. Let us examine a few.

LANGUAGE OF PRAYER

Unfortunately, when we talk about languages of prayer, we limit it to speaking in tongues or tears; but there are many others. Prayer is communication between men and their supreme being.

---

3. https://www.assistiveware.com/blog/the-power-of-language

Both man and God express thoughts through various means of expression. The supreme God understands every language spoken by the unlearnt, literate, mute, and deaf. Prayer is one of the most, if not the most priceless yet free channels of communication. It is the channel of communication orchestrated by God through which He the Creator dialogues with man, His creation.

This is not limited to humans. In the book of Jonah, God spoke to the fish, and it obeyed and swallowed and then spat out Jonah. Although no words were spoken by the fish, its obedience in actions, communicated instruction received and understood - message conveyed. In the language of prayer, God utilizes not only the five natural senses but also the spiritual ones (senses). The ability to utilize spiritual senses even when natural senses fail is a powerful prayer language tool.

Apostle Joshua Selman highlighted this truth from the account of Saul's encounter in the book of Acts 9:12. Saul was physically blind, yet he saw by way of a vision Ananias putting his hand on him, so his physical sight may be restored. In the physical, they led him by the hand, but in the spiritual, vision directed him to restoration. God spoke to Saul through vision, and he understood. In vs 9 of Acts 9, communication took place between God and Ananias.

LANGUAGE OF GIVING

Sadly, the language of giving has not been taught in its entirety. For the most part, the language of giving is limited to that of tithes and offering, with the emphasized scripture being Malachi 3:8-12, which captures the possibility of man robbing God and bringing one's tithes into the storehouse; however, this is limited. In Matthew 26:7 we see Jesus being anointed with the gift of precious ointment and In Leviticus 1: 3, the instructions of burnt offering were given, which was, one male from the herd which must be offered voluntarily.

There are other scriptures regarding burnt offerings, but none stipulate more than one animal be sacrificed. However, although that was the inherited requirement unto God, which when observed expressed obedience, Solomon spoke at a higher dimension. According to 2 Chronicles 1: 6-12: *"And Solomon went up thither to the brazen altar before the LORD, which was at the tabernacle of the congregation, and offered a thousand burnt offerings upon it. In that night did God appear unto Solomon, and said unto him, 'Ask what I shall give thee.' And Solomon said unto God, 'Thou hast shewed great mercy unto David my father, and hast made me to reign in his stead. Now, O LORD God, let thy*

promise unto David my father be established: for thou hast made me
king over a people like the dust of the earth in multitude. Give me now
wisdom and knowledge that I may go out and come in before this
people: for who can judge this thy people that is so great?' And God
said to Solomon, 'Because this was in thine heart, and thou hast not
asked riches, wealth, or honour, nor the life of thine enemies, neither
yet hast asked long life; but hast asked wisdom and knowledge for
thyself, that thou mayest judge my people, over whom I have made thee
king: wisdom and knowledge are granted unto thee; and I will give thee
riches, and wealth, and honour, such as none of the kings have had
that have been before thee, neither shall there any after thee have the
like."

Solomon communicated to God at a dimension that was not required but welcomed. Solomon gave a gift which was a non-obligatory tribute or token. It was not a reward nor a bribe, but a communication of love. He crossed over from the prescribed required sacrifices and spoke at a level that was not common. He migrated from the language of one to that of thousands. God is a master of languages. Whatever dimension you communicate with Him, He will respond. Therefore, God will not respond in the language 'one' when you pray in the language 'a Thousand.' Solomon communicated at an uncommon level, and it got God's attention - He responded in a like manner. The norm is that the human asks God for his/her desire but at this level of communication, God does the asking. Solomon responded. God said, based on your level of expression, which was more than I required, I will do more for you than you asked. We cross over with this truth that was expressed by Pastor Morris, "you can never outgive God." God will never allow you to outspeak Him. Solomon's level of communication opened unto him possibilities never imagined. His motive was pure. He did not increase his sacrifice with the tone of forcing God's hand. This is critical to note. Solomon was simply in love with God. He spoke from a place of sincere love for God.

The dimension at which you communicate with God will become the standard by which humans communicate with you. Solomon's fame became known and in 2 Chronicles 9, we see the Queen of Sheba visiting him. See verse 1: *"And when the queen of Sheba heard of the fame of Solomon, she came to prove Solomon with hard questions at Jerusalem, with a very great company, and camels that bare spices, and gold in abundance, and precious stones..."* And then verse 9: *"And she gave the king an hundred and twenty talents of gold, and of spices great abundance, and precious stones: neither was there any such spice as the queen of Sheba gave king Solomon."*

The queen of Sheba communicated with her gifts which were by what she was told of him. He gave to God like never before and she gave spices unto him, like never before. Queen of Sheba crossed over into a realm of understanding that few have trod. You must communicate at the dimension of the person you are communicating with.

Reciprocation is a powerful tool used in the language of giving. You will receive by your giving. A major error that is made as communication takes place in the language of giving is the belief that quantity equals quality. Jesus expressed this truth in the account of Mark 12:41-44. Both the rich and the poor gave into the treasury. The rich out of their abundance and a poor widow gave two mites. Jesus said the widow gave more than the rich because she gave all she had. Some will hastily question Jesus' position.

However, it takes me back to the story of the pig and the chicken. Both were required to contribute to a fundraiser. The chicken gave some eggs and went its merry way feeling proud of its contribution, the pig was not so chirpy. For it to give pork chops, it required everything it had, which was its life. There are giving and there are giving. The reality is there is a message embedded in every gift. Your gift speaks volumes. Therefore, you must examine carefully the message associated with your gifts. We remember in the book of Genesis; Cain's gift was rejected while Abel's gift was accepted by God. Two gifts bearing two different messages.

LANGUAGE OF MONEY

Money is a daily language that unfortunately many do not have mastery over. A major part of child-rearing should be teachings in the language of money. According to Proverbs 22: 6-7, *"Train up a child in the way he should go, and when he is old, he will not depart from it. The rich rule over the poor, and the borrower is a servant to the lender."*

These two verses have indebted implications which have been ignored for ages. How can a poor parent train a child in a language that he/she is poverty-stricken in? Also, note that the rich lend to the poor making the poor perpetual servant to the rich.

MONEY COMMANDS HOW THE WORLD COMMUNICATES TO YOU

Years ago, I traded female clothing. Sometimes I shopped alone, other times I would shop with my brother. My brother and I commanded two different dimensions of monetary communication. "I went into a store and inquired about the price of a dozen blouses. The store clerk quoted $48. When I asked for a discount, he said that was the best price. My brother entered the store, and I showed him the blouses. After examining them, he approached the salesclerk. Instead of asking about the price, he inquired about how many dozens of blouses were in a box. The clerk answered four. My brother then asked, 'What's the best price per box?' The clerk replied, '$44 per dozen.' After some negotiation, my brother said, 'Give me two boxes at $36 per dozen.' The clerk, seemingly exasperated, countered, 'You're killing me! I'll let them go for $39.' We purchased the blouses. While I communicated at the level of a dozen, my brother negotiated at the level of boxes." My communication did not command the respect of negotiation.

It is said that an empty barrel makes the most noise, but in the language of money, the deeper your pocket, the louder you speak. For the poor man, poverty is like a spirit of muteness, it dumbs the voice of the poor. The book of Ecclesiastes tells us that money answers all things- (temporal sense). This solidifies the muteness of the poor; the lack of money has rendered the poor answerless. It means life has presented the poor with many questions that they cannot afford to answer. In the absence of the ability to communicate effectively or at a level that commands respect, the answerless person will flee the language of money and resort to another language.

Communication between the language of money and demonstration. A company that is doing great financially shuns the low echoes of the staff as they cry relentlessly for salary increases and improved benefits. The staff seeks communication at a dimension that they command no respect, but their demonstration speaks loudly. Each hour they stay off the job, the company loses valuable communication power (money). The demonstration is not what the company will respond to but the money that it is losing.

As you Cross Over into your better, you reject being limited to communication only by written languages. Recently I received a mighty deliverance as I came to a greater understanding of a simple truth. Money is not evil, but the love of money is. I needed money but because of a dwarfed monetary concept, I ignorantly did not appreciate money as a response to the demands of life.

I never knew I could pray for money. Now with greater comprehension, I know I must pursue the wealth of other languages. Be determined to grow in the knowledge and expertise of the language of money. Mature financially to greater dimensions in your monetary voice. Cultivate and position yourself to be ready with the answers to life's many questions. Acquisition of money will require knowledge of stewardship. The old proverb says a fool and his money shall part. Both the rich and the poor speak the language of money but on different levels. The poor consume more than that which is invested. One way of shifting the level of monetary communication is to desist from consuming seeds needed for planting. No seeds planted; no fruit harvested.

LANGUAGE OF THE "BLOOD"

Many persons are of the view that the first time we hear of blood in the Bible is from the following: Genesis 3:21 *"Unto Adam also and to his wife did the LORD God make coats of skins and clothed them."*

They conclude that God killed an animal and used its skin to make a covering for man. In my submission, I do not see that from scripture. I see that God made them coats of skin. That is it. The scripture did not tell me where or what He made it from. I do not know if He spoke it into being. For me, the first place I see the word blood is, Genesis 4:9-11: *"And the LORD said unto Cain, where is Abel thy brother? And he said, I know not: Am I my brother's keeper? And he said, what hast thou done? The voice of thy brother's blood crieth unto me from the ground. And now art thou cursed from the earth, which hath opened her mouth to receive thy brother's blood from thy hand."*

From Genesis 4:9-11, we learn some powerful truths about the blood. Let's cross over to these truths:

#1. Blood has a voice, #2. Blood cries, #3 the blood can get God's attention, and #4. The blood is received by the earth.

The blood spoke a language that God understood; Cain was not aware of the possibility of this communication. He thought hiding the body of Abel was sufficient. However, the blood spoke, and God heard. A body was hidden but the blood cried. The blood cried unto God. Was it that the blood told the story of what happened, or it cried to be avenged? Look at the vast expanse of who God is. He hears the very cry of the blood. Why then are you doubting that He hears your prayers? That was the first murder, and the earth received the shed blood. Since then, countless amounts of murders and bloodshed have taken place, and yes, I truly believe the earth is still opening its mouth and receiving. Please look at the following.

See Matthew 26:26-28:

"And as they were eating, Jesus took bread, and blessed it, and broke it, and gave it to the disciples, and said, Take, eat; this is my body. And he took the cup, and gave thanks, and gave it to them, saying,

Drink ye all of it; for this is my blood of the New Testament, which is shed for many for the remission of sins."

Jesus made it clear; His blood is the life that is shed. The people saw only blood, not life. When we take communion, we do so in remembrance of his life that was shed. Jesus was crucified and his blood shed for our sins. He paid the debt mankind could not pay. Pay close attention, Abel's blood cried unto God and He heard it, what is the blood of Jesus communicating about you?

The blood of Jesus has spoken on your behalf, but many are not clear or have not come into full knowledge of what it has said. As a result, we have not stood our ground in agreement with what has been spoken. The power of agreement is a serious cross-over truth. You need to come into agreement with what the blood of Jesus has spoken about you. Jesus spoke about an agreement in Matthew 18:19, *"Again I say unto you, that if two of you shall agree on earth as touching anything that they shall ask, it shall be done for them of my Father which is in heaven."*

The above verse gives us a clear indication of the power of agreement. Now, think about the wealth, power, and possibilities you would realize if you truly began to agree with the blood of Jesus and what it has spoken about you. Please give your attention to a few of what has been spoken, so you can be strategic in your agreement with the spoken words of the blood of Jesus.

Cancellation: Romans 8:1, *"There is therefore now no condemnation to them which are in Christ Jesus, who walk not after the flesh, but after the Spirit."*

The blood cancelled all manner of condemnation. Cross over with this - if you carry your past with you, it becomes your present! Your present does not have to be a replica of your past. You are a new creation in Christ Jesus. It matters not the number of abortions you have done, how many extramarital affairs you have been a part of, the countless lies, and cheating that you committed nor how much drugs you have put in your body. As a believer in Jesus, you are a new person. Please be cognizant of this truth, not even the witchcraft you participated in, is enough to separate you from the love of God. Today it is imperative that you crucify shame, guilt, and regrets of your past sins. You had a sexual relationship with your best friend's partner a few years ago and every time you see your friend, you still feel guilty, and ashamed. Wait, has not Jesus forgiven you? It is no longer an issue. It is done.

I have seen people beautify themselves through nice dressing, hair grooming, jewelry, etc. they wear them beautifully. Question: why are you wearing shame and guilt and fear?

What beauty do they add to you? My past was my continued truth until I rejected it. Listen; there are things that will remain loyally married to you until you decide to divorce them. Divorce is not restricted to separation between a husband and wife. It must expand to separation between humans and unhealthy possibilities. The possibilities that invoke negatives must be divorced. Let today be the beginning of you disrobing yourself of the past clothing that represents your sins. In the account of Genesis 32:6-7, we see one brother's past haunting him as he feared the repercussions of his past wrongs done to his brother:

"And the messengers returned to Jacob, saying, 'We came to thy brother Esau, and also, he cometh to meet thee, and four hundred men with him.' Then Jacob was greatly afraid and distressed: and he divided the people that was with him, and the flocks, and herds, and the camels, into two bands".

Jacob was afraid because of the evil he did to his brother in the past. By the instructions of his mother, he deceived his father and received his brother's blessing. Years later he must face his fear. Esau did swear that after his father's death, he would kill Jacob, his brother.

Like Jacob, you will be confronted with the actions of your past, but the challenge is, how you conduct yourselves. Do you allow them to dictate your now? Cross-over with this truth, if you allow your past to bully you, you will forever live defeated in your present. Revelation 12:11 tells us that we overcome by the blood of the lamb (Jesus). Whatever the action or deed of the past we should repent and never go back to those lifestyles. Humility plays a vital role in us overcoming the struggle with sin. Please remember you are now beautiful because of the blood of Jesus.

LOCATION

Ephesians 2:4-6 states, *"But God, who is rich in mercy, for his great love wherewith he loved us, even when we were dead in sins, hath quickened us together with Christ, (by grace ye are saved;) And hath raised us up together and made us sit together in heavenly places in Christ Jesus."*

Please give attention to this powerful truth; because of the blood of Jesus, your location is now in heavenly places. If you grasp this, many battles you would fight, you will ignore because they are at a lower location. A major mistake you make is forsaking your location and abiding at a lower level. An excellent example of this truth is seen in the book of Revelation. See Revelations 12:7-9: *"And there was war in heaven: Michael and his angels fought against the dragon, and the dragon fought with his angels and prevailed not; neither was their place found anymore in* heaven. And the great dragon was cast out, that old serpent, called the Devil, and Satan, which deceiveth the whole world: he was cast out into the earth, and his angels were cast out with him."

Notice the war was caused because Satan wanted to reign, to boot out God. He challenged God's authority, yet in the fight, we do not see God. Satan is below God's level. If God had gotten involved in the fight, it would be a promotion for Satan. God ignored him and allowed Michael to handle the situation. Cross over in this wise, there are situations you need to not get involved in. They are below your grade. Many believers fail to realize that sometimes doing nothing is the best thing one can do. This is what God did. He never allowed himself to be pulled into a fight with Satan. Satan received a nothing action from God. The phrase 'to pay attention' is commonly used, but we must realize that whenever we address or respond to something, we are actually 'paying' with our attention. It costs us to shift our focus.

See Mathew 27:13-14, "...Then Pilate asked Him, *"Do You not hear how many charges they are bringing against you?"* But Jesus did not answer, not even to a single charge, much to the governor's amazement."

After Michael defeats Satan, watch what happens in Jude 1:9, *"Yet Michael the archangel, when contending with the devil he*

disputed about the body of Moses, durst not bring against him a
railing accusation, but said, The Lord rebuke thee."

Michael said, in other words, I have defeated you already, no need for a rematch. He went straight to the higher source and rebuked him from that higher level and rank. Here lies a major problem-you have been fighting the same match repeatedly. Same devil, same opposition, same situations, which is nothing more than mismanagement of time and resources. The enemy understands if he can bombard you with fighting at a low level, you will never cross over to the victories of higher levels that await you. Know and function from your place of location.

HEALED

Isaiah 53:5 says, "But he was wounded for our transgressions, he was bruised for our iniquities: the chastisement of our peace was upon him, and with his stripes we are healed."

The blood of Jesus has declared you healed. This is a key testament, nonetheless, one needs to come into agreement with the blood of Jesus to be healed. God's sovereign will is already established and requires submission before the full benefits of His will be manifested in your life. Please understand that any sickness that is prevailing now in the life of the believer is an indication of the operation of a lie. Either the scripture is not the truth, that by the blood of Jesus, you are healed, or the sickness is lying that it has legal rights to occupy. You might question Job's sickness against the above statement, which is good. Please note that the sickness did not prevail over Job as he was restored. The blood already spoke loud and clear. Its words cannot be cancelled. Pay close attention to the language used. By His stripes (Blood released) you are healed (not will be healed) but already healed. God is waiting for you to activate your faith with confidence and grasp that which Jesus has already done for you. Whose voice will we adhere to or believe? The Blood's voice or an infirmity voice?

NEW CREATURE

The blood says in 2 Corinthians 5:17, *"Therefore if any man be in Christ, he is a new creature: old things are passed away; behold, all things have become new."* Wait, do we understand what the word new means? According to the Merriam-Webster Dictionary new means, not existing before; made, introduced, or discovered recently.

As a new creature, you must discover who you are. The Blood has positioned you on a path of discovery. Who are you? In discovering yourself, it is advised that the position that Paul the Apostle took should be copied- Philippians 3:8, *"Yet indeed I also count all things loss for the excellence of the knowledge of Christ Jesus*

47

my Lord, for whom I have suffered the loss of all things, and count them as rubbish, that I may gain Christ." You are a new creature by the blood of Jesus being discovered. Because you are a new creature, you do not need to imitate anyone. Being different is not necessarily a bad thing; being special does not mean you are odd/weird/strange. God created you. If He wanted a replica of someone else, He would have created that. He created you. Be you!

Persons and spirits are searching for you but are unable to locate you because the Blood of Jesus has relocated you. You are not at the place they once saw you. Watch what Jesus said in John 11:43-44, *"And when he thus had spoken, he cried with a loud voice, Lazarus, come forth. And he that was dead came forth, bound hand and foot with grave clothes: and his face was bound about with a napkin. Jesus saith unto them, loose him, and let him go."*

When Lazarus returned from the grave, he came without the sickness that took his life. This is how the blood of Jesus Works. It is not just resurrection from death to life, but everything that participated or contributed to your previous state must be removed. New location through the blood.

---

1.   https://faothewolfgirl.wordpress.com/

DEBT FREE

We read in Genesis 37:26-32, *"And Judah said unto his brethren, what profit is it if we slay our brother, and conceal his blood? Come, and let us sell him to the Ishmaelites, and let not our hand be upon him; for he is our brother and our flesh. And his brethren were content. Then there passed by Midianites merchantmen, and they drew and lifted up Joseph out of the pit and sold Joseph to the Ishmaelites for twenty pieces of silver: and they brought Joseph into Egypt. And they took Joseph's coat, and killed a kid of the goats, and dipped the coat in the blood, and they sent the coat of many colours, and they brought it to their father; and said, 'This have we found: know now whether it be thy son's coat or no."*

Joseph's brothers sold him, killed a goat then dipped his coat in its blood and presented it to their father as a testimony that wild animals might have killed him. The blood that was shed was used to deceive Jacob and to hide the truth of their actions. However, the blood of Jesus speaks the complete truth concerning you. Like Joseph, Jesus was sold, and blood was shed. A major difference is Jesus was the ram slain. His blood was shed. Right before He died, He spoke the truth concerning you. Let's look at John 19:30, *"When Jesus therefore had received the vinegar, he said, it is finished: and he bowed his head, and gave up the ghost."*

What was finished? His assignment, the reason He came. Which was to redeem mankind. What does redeem mean? **Redeem:** gain or regain possession of (something) in exchange for payment.

In other words, the blood/life of Jesus was used as payment for your sins. The blood has regained you unto God the Father. Your sin's debt has been paid in full. You are no longer a debtor to sin. The blood/life of Jesus declares you free from all the covenants you had with Satan.

Do you understand that you are free? This is very important for you to learn and hold on to. The enemy will always be digging up your past sins to claim rights over you. One day I was at church worshipping and the enemy began reminding me of the sins of my past, it affected me until I completely crossed over to the truth that I had been forgiven.

Please understand that the enemy is a thief. He tries to collect on the same debt as many times as possible. He is collecting on a debt that Jesus paid in full by the shedding and giving of His blood and life. A position we must embrace and promote is, paid in full! This resonates in my spirit; Satan desires to collect on a debt that has already been cleared. Cross over in this delivering truth, you owe Satan nothing. (No-Thing). The blood of Jesus has declared you are debt free so start living as such.

Please look at these life-changing verses; Romans 8:2, *"For the law of the Spirit of life in Christ Jesus hath made me free from the law of sin and death."* Romans 8:33, *"Who shall lay anything to the charge of God's elect? It is God that justifieth."* Romans 5:10, *"For if, when we were enemies, we were reconciled to God by the death of his Son, much more, being reconciled, we shall be saved by his life."*

I remember when I got saved: for days I kept singing the song, "I am free, praise the Lord I am free, I'm no longer bound, no more chains holding me, my soul is resting, it's just a blessing, praise the Lord, hallelujah I'm free". I received freedom through the shed Blood of Jesus. The Blood declares me free.

Now you have crossed over to this powerful truth, some people are not happy. Some persons have been employed by the kingdom of darkness to function as debt collectors, but commencing today, they shall die of hunger, the debt collection staff has been made redundant.

There is another position that has been made redundant-grave diggers. Everything that you have buried, the gravediggers are searching for, but they will be confronted by the Blood of Jesus. You have buried and left your past errors and sins in the cemetery, but grave diggers are searching for your past stories.

THE BLOOD SPEAKS VICTORY

Revelation 12:10-11 says: *"And I heard a loud voice saying in heaven, Now is come salvation, and strength, and the kingdom of our God, and the power of his Christ: for the accuser of our brethren is cast down, which accused them before our God day and night. And they overcame him by the blood of the Lamb, and by the word of their testimony, and they loved not their lives unto the death."*

The word overcame speaks to the past tense. It means it is already done-already won. Some time ago I crossed over into this transformational revelation which I now share with you. You are not fighting to win, because the victory is already yours through the work of Jesus. Therefore, you are living your secured victory. Never belittle this truth; the Blood of Jesus has guaranteed your perpetual winning seasons. You never lose; you are always winning.

Is this true? How can you say I'm always winning when I'm barely keeping my head above the water? Even when it looks like you have lost, you are winning. As mentioned earlier, the Hebrew boys in Daniel chapter three said that if God delivers us, we win, and if He chooses not to deliver us, we still win. Cross over to this acceptance, as a child of God, you always win, even if not in this temporal life. According to Paul, (death for the believer) is not a loss, but gain.

The Blood of Jesus speaks equality: this truth is substantiated by the following scriptures.

Galatians 3:28, *"There is neither Jew nor Greek, there is neither bond nor free, there is neither male nor female: for ye are all one in Christ Jesus."*

1 Corinthians 12:12-13, *"For as the body is one, and hath many members, and all the members of that one body, being many, are one body: so also, is Christ. For by one Spirit are we all baptized into one body, whether we be Jews or Gentiles, whether we be bond or free; and have been all made to drink into one Spirit."*

Unfortunately, this truth of equality has been massacred. There is an illegal practice, based on kingdom principles of elevating one person over the other because of factors such as titles, manifested gifts, and financial or social standings. Cross over to this truth; you are not better than your brother nor your sister and neither is any better than you.

Some people are made to believe that if they do not speak in tongues, they are less than those who do. Or if you did not go to Bible College, you are less than those who attended. Embrace this truth, the Blood speaks equality. The same access your pastor has to God is the same access you have to Him. Access for the rich and the poor, the intelligent and the illiterate, for the white, black, Hispanic, Asian, etc. is the same. The person who gives ten dollars (10) tithe is equal to the one who gives a thousand (1000). The inequality we are seeing among humans is not from God. He is constant, He has no favourites. The inequality is from brothers and sisters incited by Satan. Regrettably, we have been allowing the enemy to use us against each other.

I remember talking to a pastor and someone came and interrupted our conversation, the person proceeded to address the pastor as though I was invisible. Another time I visited a church, not as a walk-in visitor but as Rev. Morrison. It is sad how differently I was treated; same person, yet Rev. Morrison is treated far better than Brother Morrison, this needs to stop. You must cross over to this imperative truth- treat each other equally, despite statuses. We are exhorted by the writer of the book of James:

"If ye fulfil the royal law according to the scripture, Thou shalt love thy neighbour as thyself, ye do well: But if ye have respect to persons, ye commit sin, and are convinced of the law as transgressors." (James 2:8-9)

How many of you are guilty? The Blood declares you equal. If the Prophet, Pastor, or Teacher can be taken to the five-star hotel for dinner, then the gardener and the church cleaner can be taken to the same. Some may dispute this crossover truth citing the words of Paul in 1 Timothy 5:17, where he spoke of some labourers deserving of double honor. However, look at how Paul pens this truth in the book of Romans.

Romans 8:17, *"And if children, then heirs; heirs of God, and joint heirs with Christ; if so be that we suffer with him, that we may be also glorified together."*

By the shed blood of Jesus, we are made joint heirs with him. Yet you do not treat each other as equals. Please let this transform how you treat each other; the blood declares you equal.

THE BLOOD MAKES US RIGHTEOUS

A simple definition of righteousness is right standing. However, as you think of yourself, you must never forget that your standing before God is like filthy rags. The prophet Isaiah speaks on our righteousness in this light:

"But we are all as an unclean thing, and all our righteousness are as filthy rags, and we all do fade as a leaf; and our iniquities, like the wind, have taken us away." (Isaiah 64:6)

You must rejoice knowing that because of the blood of Jesus, God does not see you by your filth but through the righteousness of Jesus. Jesus' shed blood speaks loudly and has declared you righteous. Cross over to this undefeated truth, you are in right standing with God.

CROSS OVER KEYS

1. Prayer is one of the most, if not the most priceless yet free channels of communication.

2. In the language of prayer, God utilizes not only the five natural senses but also the spiritual ones.

3. The ability to utilize spiritual senses even when natural senses fail is a powerful prayer language tool.

4. God is a master of languages. Whatever dimension you communicate with him, He will respond.

5. You can never outgive God." God will never allow you to outspeak Him.

6. The dimension at which you communicate with God will become the standard by which humans communicate with you.

7. You must communicate at the dimension of the person you are communicating with.

8. Reciprocation is a powerful tool used in the language of giving.

9. You will receive in accordance with your giving.

10. A major error that is made as communication takes place in the language of giving is the belief that quantity equates to quality.

11. There are giving and there are giving. The reality is there is a message embedded in every gift.

12. It is said that an empty barrel makes the most noise, but in the language of money, the deeper your pocket, the louder you speak.

13. Reject being limited to communication only by written languages.

14. Be determined to grow in the knowledge and expertise of the language of money.

15. Mature financially to greater dimensions in your monetary voice.

16. Acquisition of money will require knowledge of stewardship.

17. One way of shifting the level of monetary communication is to desist from consuming seeds needed for planting. No seeds planted; no fruit harvested.

18. You need to agree with what the blood of Jesus has spoken about you.

19. If you carry your past with you, it becomes your present!

20. There are situations you need to not get involved in. They are below your grade.

21. Know and function from your place of location.

22. A position we must embrace and promote is, paid in full!

23. You are not fighting to win, because the victory is already yours through the work of Jesus.

CHAPTER FOUR
UNDER REVIEW

Last year as I searched for some products on Amazon, my lack of knowledge made it difficult to choose among the beautiful, displayed products; but the reviews helped me greatly. The reviews were from customers who had experience with the various products. The reviewers shared their testimonies, some were good, others damning. The truth is as humans; we too are being reviewed. We are scrutinized by the world, our peers, and by the Word of God. It is true, that the word of God is our biggest reviewer.

In every review lies certain key elements: the object, expectations, and result. Every reviewer has a scorecard, from which they can check the boxes as to how he/she measures up to a given criteria. An excellent method of reviewing is that of peers.

REVIEW OF PEERS

"There was a certain man in Caesarea called Cornelius, a centurion of the band called the Italian band, a devout man, and one that feared God with all his house, which gave much alms to the people, and prayed to God always." (Acts 10:1-2)

What a beautiful review - devout, feared God, gave alms to the people, and prayed to God always.

Daniel came under review from his peers who were his enemies.

"Then the presidents and princes sought to find occasion against Daniel concerning the kingdom, but they could find no occasion nor fault; forasmuch as he was faithful, neither was there any error or fault found in him. Then said these men, we shall not find any occasion against this Daniel, except we find it against him concerning the law of his God." (Daniel 6:4-5)

When they reviewed Daniel's file, they found no fault or error; my God, what an example for us to follow; that place where your enemies cannot find anything on you is not achieved overnight or is it an easy walk in the park. Let this be your desire- cross over to where your enemies' review of you is, he/she is a Man or Woman of God.

It is admirable when your peers call you a man of God but it's a different level when your enemies acknowledge you as a child of the King; this was no small achievement by Daniel. Look closer.

"In the third year of the reign of Jehoiakim king of Judah came Nebuchadnezzar king of Babylon unto Jerusalem and besieged it. And

the Lord gave Jehoiakim king of Judah into his hand, with part of the vessels of the house of God: which he carried into the land of Shinar to the house of his god; and he brought the vessels into the treasure house of his god...Now among these were of the children of Judah, Daniel, Hananiah, Mishael, and Azariah." (Daniel 1:1-2:6)

Daniel was not exhibiting excellence in a place he was familiar with, but rather a place where he was a stranger. He was captured and taken into a foreign land with foreign gods and practices, this is where Daniel's review was written. It was not written within the church but from the house of heathens. What is your conduct outside the eyesight and hearing of your church and family setting?

REVIEWS FROM GOD AND SATAN

"And the LORD said unto Satan, Hast thou considered my servant Job, that there is none like him in the earth, a perfect and an upright man, one that feareth God, and escheweth evil? Then Satan answered the LORD, and said, Doth Job fear God for nought? Hast not thou made a hedge about him, and about his house, and about all that he hath on every side? thou hast blessed the work of his hands, and his substance is increased in the land." (Job 1:8-10)

We rejoice at our earthly enemies acknowledging that we are children of God, but nothing beats a good review from God. God said about Job; he is my servant (priceless), there is none like him on the earth. Wait, not just in the area where he lived, but even beyond. Perfect, upright, fears God, and eschewed evil. This was from God. The perfect God who sees and knows everything says, you are perfect; what a review! While you appreciate the good reviews from men, be purpose to not stop there, but to cross over to receiving great reviews from God. If the good reviews are only from men, we have failed. What has God said about you?

Then comes Satan trying to demean God's review with one of his own. It is true that Satan is allowed to speak against you. Satan says, "Job is simply having a great review because of the provisions God had put in place for him". In other words, "God, this good review is not because of Job, but because of you. Is Satan right when he accuses you of only serving God because you are blessed?

The question is, 'What will your review be when you are under pressure?' Here is a powerful crossover key; the strength of a man is known not in the good times but in seasons of adversities. A popular saying is pressure burst pipes and pressure pushes water uphill. When you experience significant pressure, you decide the outcome. You either burst under the intensity of the weight or you dig deep into your inner strength and capture the victory that awaits you.

A daughter of mine went through such pressure that she could not buy food for her son. She had to collect the remains from the cafeteria at work (in the name of her dog), take it home, and prepare it for her son and herself for dinner; this was serious pressure. What magnified the pressure was the self-invited rescuers who rode in on their shiny modern horses. The reality was, that they presented a barter which was not in keeping with righteous practices, financial provision in exchange for her body. Despite her needs and the unholy provisions, she completed that journey with excellent reviews. Please understand that a product built to withstand hurricane-force winds cannot get verification until a hurricane passes. The review begins as the hurricane starts until it's finished. What category of storm are you built to survive?

After you have gone through your crisis, then you can add the following to your review.

PRACTICES

In writing this book, I realized a dogma I held on to dearly has changed. I previously held the belief that good time reviews are not to be considered worthy for appraisals but rather your under pressure, about to drown, clothes on fire reviews. However, I have learned that good times can be as dangerous as bad times. It would not be a small indictment to disregard the reviews in good weather. As you journey on life's terrain, you will come to appreciate the various weather systems afforded unto us. Rainy days are as vital as sunny ones. Cross over in this wise, if all you have are either good or bad days, you cannot be completely reviewed. How is your relationship with God during the good seasons? How are you in gratitude, thanksgiving, and in prayer? Do you fast in the good times?

The truth is that not everyone gets good reviews from God. Let's look! In the book of 1 Samuel chapter 16, God said to Samuel the prophet, that He has rejected Saul from being king over Israel. Saul was anointed and appointed the king of Israel, but he failed and was rejected by heaven. Saul, as a human being was not rejected but his leadership or kingship was, God made that abundantly clear. God said I have rejected him from reigning over Israel. A major continuous error that is made is preserving the notion that once anointed for a position, always appointed. Saul's anointing for the position of king ended before his appointment, without his knowledge. There were two standards which he needed to be in sync - heaven and earth. On earth, he was the king, but from heaven he was a reject. TD Jakes said God is the only one who fires you and lets you keep your office.

Saul's rejection was the consequence of his disobedience. We have undervalued the power and wealth of obedience. Obedience is a major retainer of appointment factors. Duration is immediately linked to obedience. Obedience is easily the highest form of worship to God. Cross over with this truth, your true wealth is not measured on the economic scale of the world but upon your level of obedience to God. Unfortunately, many persons over harvest Romans 11:29 which states, *"For the gifts and calling of God are without repentance"*. They should temper this with Revelations 2:1-6:

"Unto the angel of the church of Ephesus write; These things saith he that holdeth the seven stars in his right hand, who walketh in the midst of the seven golden candlesticks; I know thy works, and thy labour, and thy patience, and how thou canst not bear them which are evil: and thou hast tried them which say they are apostles, and are not, and hast found them liars: And hast borne, and hast patience, and for my name's sake hast laboured, and hast not fainted. Nevertheless, I have somewhat against thee because thou hast left thy first love. Remember therefore from whence thou art fallen, and repent, and do the first works; or else I will come unto thee quickly, and will remove thy candlestick out of his place, except thou repent. But this thou hast, that thou hatest the deeds of the Nicolaitans, which I also hate."

The review of the church at Ephesus was a mixed one. By human standards, you would praise the church because of its history. However, please look at what God had to say according to Revelation 2: 1- 5:

"Unto the angel of the church of Ephesus write; These things saith he that holdeth the seven stars in his right hand, who walketh in the midst of the seven golden candlesticks; I know thy works, and thy labour, and thy patience, and how thou canst not bear them which are evil: and thou hast tried them which say they are apostles and are not, and hast found them liars: And hast borne, and hast patience, and for my name's sake hast laboured, and hast not fainted. Nevertheless, I have somewhat against thee because thou hast left thy first love. Remember therefore from whence thou art fallen, and repent, and do the first works; or else I will come unto thee quickly, and will remove thy candlestick out of his place, except thou repent."

We are constantly under review. But one review we often neglect is, self-review.

The Holy Spirit who dwells within us, is not blind nor deaf to our daily activities. I like what the scripture says. Let's look:

"Examine yourselves, whether ye be in the faith; prove your own selves. Know ye not your own selves, how that Jesus Christ is in you,

except ye be reprobates? But I trust that ye shall know that we are not reprobates. Now I pray to God that ye do no evil; not that we should appear approved, but that ye should do that which is honest, though we be as reprobates." (2 Corinthians 13:5-7) Look at Paul, hear what he said as he reviewed himself:

"But watch thou in all things, endure afflictions, do the work of an evangelist, make full proof of thy ministry. For I am now ready to be offered, and the time of my departure is at hand. I have fought a good fight, I have finished my course, I have kept the faith:" (2 Timothy 4:5-7)

Paul's review of himself was awesome. It said no regrets. There are times when I know I failed in a presented situation. I did not act by the will of God. The truth is that the will of God is not always easy to follow.

A young lady shared the following with me, "There is a taxi that I have been taking for years, the driver's wife is a Christian, but he is not. Over the years he constantly brags about his praying wife and people better mind how dem fight against him because him will tell him wife and she will pray, and God will deal with dem case." He always talks about his praying wife. He is not saved but his review of his wife is priceless. Let us be conscious that we are constantly being reviewed.

CROSS OVER KEYS

1. Cross over to where your enemies' review of you is; He/she is a Man or Woman of God.

2. We rejoice at our earthly enemies acknowledging that we are children of God, but nothing beats a good review from God.

3. The strength of a man is known not in the good times but in seasons of adversities.

4. Please understand that a product built to withstand hurricane-force winds cannot get verification until a hurricane passes.

5. Rainy days are as vital as sunny ones. Cross over in this wise, if all you have are sunny days, the nozzle of the gun is right at your head.

6. You have undervalued the power and wealth of obedience.

7. Obedience is easily the highest form of worship to God.

8. Obedience is a major retainer of appointment factor. Duration is immediately linked to obedience.

9. Your true wealth is not measured on the economic scale of the world but upon your level of obedience to God.

10. Be conscious that you are constantly being reviewed.

CHAPTER FIVE
I DO NOT LOOK LIKE WHAT I HAVE BEEN THROUGH

In 2018 a dear friend of mine was in a motor vehicle accident

which resulted in her then-recently acquired vehicle being destroyed. The insurance company rendered the vehicle written off. If your insurer considers the cost of repairs to be uneconomical, your car will be classed as an insurance write-off. Uneconomical repairs would cost 50%-60% of the vehicle's value, but this could be even lower for a brand-new vehicle. In other words, it would cost more to be repaired than to discard. My friend shared two pictures with me, which expressed the crash and after states of the same vehicle. The truth is the mangled-looking state was never the original look, but life happens. Has life crashed you beyond recognition? Do you feel as though there is no place for recovery or restoration? The mangled vehicle was not retained by the original owners as it was assessed and deemed too expensive to be repaired. They opted out of the option of restoration and embraced separation. Please cross over into this powerful truth; there is always room for restoration.

Perhaps you have been deemed by others to be too costly to be repaired, that is the error many people made with you. They reasoned that it is cheaper to replace you than to invest in your restoration. You hate errors, however, some errors against you are necessary. According to Galatians 6:1, restoration should be pursued. It reads, *"Brethren if a man be overtaken in a fault, ye which is spiritual, restore such an one in the spirit of meekness, considering thyself, lest thou also be tempted"*. What the Bible is telling you is that the possibility of being mangled is very real. Anyone can find themselves in a state of needing repairs.

My friend agreed with the insurance company and ended the relationship she had with her vehicle; she sold it, she discarded her vehicle. Like that mangled vehicle, many of you have been the victim of being discarded. However, what if your poverty was in that thinking? The thought of being a discarded victim? Is it possible that the putting aside was indeed your blessing in disguise? Cross over with this true possibility, being disregarded was indeed a blessing in disguise.

If you were not rendered parked, you would have looked to men for your restoration. But when they assessed and deemed you irreparable, then you had no choice but to trust God. Now, because of what He has done to you, you must give Him all the glory. God knew in-spite of what you have been through, you have value. Your true value was revealed after you went through being crushed, cast aside, and then restored. An excellent place of maturity to achieve is seeing the wealth of someone during their mangled state.

It was good that they discarded you. You learned things about yourself simply because you were crushed. Look at this- the insurance company paid money to my friend for her crashed jeep. She sold it and bought a brand-new vehicle. Although her new vehicle was beautiful and luxurious, when she saw the now restored jeep, she told the new owner (the restorer) she wanted her jeep back. It's a harsh truth, but some of those who are ringing off your phones, inviting you here and there, did not want to be in your company until you were restored. They did not want to deal with you and all your issues. They saw your number on the screen and opted not to answer. They avoided you. Wait, are we guilty of the same? Have we avoided our brethren who seemed to be always in crisis? Have we gotten tired of hearing them cry? It gets deeper; who have you simply blocked because of their brokenness? You no longer see their messages or receive their calls because they are blocked.

Please, you need to rejoice because you do not look like what you have been through. You do not look like the victim of rape, physical abuse, poverty, prostitution, abortions, drug abuse, divorce, mental illness, family abandonment, many failures, depression, low self-esteem, imprisonment, and or a backslidden state. You can unapologetically say, "Do not be fooled by my demeanor, expensive clothes, the office I sit in, the family I now have.... I have my story". The wealth is- you are not what your story said you should be. You are what God says you are. If it were up to your story alone, you would certainly look like what you have been through. But God! You are not the only one who has had to be restored. Let's look at the account of Mark Chapter 5.

"And when he was come out of the ship, immediately there met him out of the tombs a man with an unclean spirit, Who had his dwelling among the tombs; and no man could bind him, no, not with chains: Because that he had been often bound with fetters and chains, and the chains had been plucked asunder by him, and the fetters broken in pieces: neither could any man tame him. And always, night and day, he was in the mountains, and in the tombs, crying, and cutting himself with stones...For he said unto him, Come out of the man, thou unclean spirit. And he asked him, what is thy name? And he answered, saying, my name is Legion: for we are many." (Mark 5:2-5, 8, 9)

"And they come to Jesus, and see him that was possessed with the devil, and had the legion, sitting, and clothed, and in his right mind:

and they were afraid… And when he was come into the ship, he that had been possessed with the devil prayed him that he might be with him. Howbeit Jesus suffered him not, but saith unto him, go home to thy friends and tell them how great things the Lord hath done for thee, and hath had compassion on thee. And he departed and began to publish in Decapolis how great things Jesus had done for him: and all men did marvel." (Mark 5:15, 18-20)

The raw truth is that if you remotely looked like what you had been through, others would not want to be in your company. You would be isolated. They saw the man clothed and in his right mind and now he was evangelizing. The people listened and marveled.

Let me list what they did not see, for clarity.

1. He had demons living within him.
2. He lived among the dead.
3. He was given supernatural strength by the demons, which he used to break chains that persons attempted to use to bind him. That means he was out of control.
4. Night and day, he cried and cut himself.
5. Demons spoke through him.
6. Not only did he have demons living in him, but he had legions (3000-6000).

While they did not mind listening to him when he was clothed and in his right mind - in his tomb state, they would never listen. Pay attention to those who visit and keep relationships with you, when you do not have it all together, those are keepers. Jesus taught a very big message about the power to care enough to restore. The possessed man did not know he had the value of evangelism until he was crushed and restored. Cross over into this truth - brokenness is a great revealer. The good times are worth knowing but the broken periods reveal deep truth.

Andre, a friend of mine, told me he went to a nearby junkyard one day. While searching for an item it occurred to him that there were a vast number of vehicles of all different makes and models, in this junkyard. All of them were designed to be driven and by design were once equipped with all that they would need to function. Yet they were now parked at a junkyard. What happened? For a multitude of reasons these vehicles were not drivable, so the owners decided that they were of limited value to them. Yet there is somebody else with a salvage yard that placed value on the same thing that was deemed junk and was willing to repurpose them to extract value. We see a powerful demonstration of this in the book of Jeremiah.

We read in Jeremiah 18:2-4:

"Arise, and go down to the potter's house, and there I will cause thee to hear my words. Then I went down to the potter's house, and, behold, he wrought a work on the wheels. And the vessel that he made of clay was marred in the hand of the potter: so, he made it again another vessel, as seemed good to the potter to make it."

There are times when vessels, even ones in the hands of the Lord, get marred; but when that happens, he does not discard the clay; point to note, the marring may be a terrible mistake you have made, a decision and the consequences thereof are just misfortune, however, while people may give up on you, God is intentional in making you another vessel. Please cross over in this wise, God has not given up on you. Based on the errors of your past, families, friends, or society might deem you a heap of junk. But be it known that God is the junkyard owner.

When humans would say I am done, a Potter has a certain grace to not only see the 'present you' but, the "you" that you can become if He is allowed to shape you. We like to say the Potter wants to put it back together again, and whilst the saying is true, it is often misunderstood. The Bible says he makes it into another vessel. Same clay but a different vessel. When you allow God to take the pieces of your broken dreams, do not expect it to go the way you planned. He is not a God of patchwork; He is into reshaping, remodeling, and repurposing. This means it may not feel right; the pieces may feel mixed up but allow God to work. As the potter repurposes you, be conscious that there are some friends which will be lost, some relationships which may not make it to the next version of you. It is time to move away from patchwork prayers. These prayers are those that are not geared towards a complete overhaul, but the fixing of patches. Cross over into this truth, your errors were necessary for you to become your best you. Did it ever occur to you that for the Potter to reshape a vessel he has to break down the existing one? Your brokenness was the necessary key to you being shaped into a masterpiece.

A big part of construction is demolition. An existing building when demolished makes room for a new structure that will best suit the modern era. You must realize that not everything you have lost is a loss. In the hands of the Potter, you are valued. You are not the sum of your mistakes.

The Potter is deliberate, and He is patient. So many times, the worry we carry is because we take full responsibility for the outcomes of so many things. If you are really in the Potter's hands, you must trust the process of the finished work. Today there is no shame in being broken. You are good clay for the hand of God. Irrespective of how long you have been walking with the Lord, you should purpose to stay on the wheel. You are still valuable to God. Cross over and learn this powerful mind elevation truth, the clay does not talk back, nor tells the Potter, I think you made an error or maybe I should be this kind of vessel instead of the one you have in mind. It is still in the hands of a competent Potter. You never hear the clay asking the potter, 'Why me?' However, we the spiritual clays question and sometimes reject God's modeling/molding of our souls.

Andre my friend said that people need to be careful of their perception and of the narrative accepted from others about yourself. He said, when he was a boy, no more than fourteen years old (14) a taxi man looked him square in the eye and said, "Anything too black nuh (is not) good". The taxi man had a perception of Andre's value which was not in cohesion with God's viewpoint. Today at thirty-three years old (33) Andre is presently an assistant VP at a national consulting firm. Cross over in this wise, your Potter is not moved by the opinions of men. It is what God says that is important. Thank God He has the final say. Whose opinion of you have you heeded concerning your end? Is that voice authorized by God to speak into your life?

CROSS OVER KEYS

1. There is always room for restoration.

2. You hate errors, however, some errors against you are necessary.

3. An excellent place of maturity to achieve is seeing the wealth of someone during their mangled state.

4. You are what God says you are. If it were up to your story alone, you would certainly look like what you have been through.

5. Pay attention to those who visit and keep relationship with you, when you do not have it all together. Those are keepers.

6. Brokenness is a great revealer. The good times are worth knowing but the broken periods reveal truth.

7. He is not a God of patchwork; He is into reshaping, remolding and repurposing.

8. Your errors were necessary for you to become your best you.

9. Your brokenness was the necessary key to you being shaped into a masterpiece.

10. You must realize that not everything we have lost is a loss.

11. The clay doesn't talk back, nor tells the Potter I think you made an error or maybe I should be this kind of vessel instead of the one you have in mind.

12. Your Potter is not moved by the opinions of men. It is what God says that is important.

CHAPTER SIX
SEIZE THE MOMENT!

This is your winning season. You cannot afford to throw it away. You have waited too long; the tides have turned in your favour, run with it. Bask in it. Facilitate no distractions. "Seize the moment." A major mistake that we make is not identifying heavenly opportunities. Heaven opens doors and we miss it. We miss it because we are not seeing through the lenses of God. We are looking for well-gift-wrapped, labelled, packages but God allows testing and trials.

A powerful necessary crossover truth is the storm is a key. It was designed to unlock the well-needed opportunity, but you were so consumed with the boisterous wind and raging sea, that you failed to see the door. Please reap the wealth of the account located in Mathew 14: 25-29:

"And when He had sent the multitudes away, He went up on the mountain by Himself to pray. Now when evening came, He was alone there. But the boat was now [b]in the middle of the sea, tossed by the waves, for the wind was contrary. Now in the fourth watch of the night Jesus went to them, walking on the sea. And when the disciples saw Him walking on the sea, they were troubled, saying, "It is a ghost!" And they cried out for fear. But immediately Jesus spoke to

them, saying, "Be of good cheer! It is I; do not be afraid." And Peter
answered Him and said, "Lord, if it is you, command me to come to
you on the water." So, He said, "Come." And when Peter had come
down out of the boat, he walked on the water to go to Jesus. But when
he saw that the wind was boisterous, he was afraid; and beginning to
sink he cried out, saying, "Lord, save me!" And immediately Jesus
stretched out His hand and caught him, and said to him, "O you of
little faith, why did you doubt?" And when they got into the boat, the
wind ceased. Then those who were in the boat came and worshiped
Him, saying, "Truly you are the Son of God."

There are several points you need to pay close attention to. Let's
highlight and expound.

1. **The storm-** Jesus, who is all-knowing sent his disciples
   to enter into the boat and sail, knowing they would
   encounter contrary winds. Please hasten to crossover
   into this truth, the contrary or opposition does not mean
   you are in the wrong or that you did not hear the voice
   of God. You must also be conscious that obedience to
   God does not neutralize any challenges. Obstacles can
   easily be an indication that you are on the right path.
   Never allow challenges faced to derail you from
   pursuing obedience to God. You might ask, why would
   Jesus intentionally send his children in the path of

storms? Looking at Luke 4: 1-2 the saints are comforted with the knowledge that Jesus Himself was led by the Holy Spirit into the wilderness to be tempted by the devil. Jesus then said as He taught His disciples to pray in Matthew 6: 13, "and lead us not into temptation." Not all leading of the Holy Spirit will be easily understood.

2. **Unchanged situation** - Jesus arrived in the storm but never interfered with it. The absence of change does not equate the nonappearance of the presence of God. This reassures you that Jesus knows where you are and what you are experiencing. Persons frequently believe they have been abandoned by God because of the raging storms of life that they are experiencing. Crossover in this wise; the presence of contrariness does not mean God is not present. He demonstrated restraint of power to bring about a greater level of belief. The ability to restrain is a greater show of power than the demonstration of might.

3. **The voice** - The disciples were afraid, they thought Jesus was a spirit until He spoke. Jesus spoke and said, "Be of good cheer it is I." Jesus said in Mathew 14:27, "My sheep listen to my voice; I know them, and they follow me." This speaks to relationships. Peter, having had a relationship with Jesus, knew His voice. Knowing the

82

voice of God is to be pursued aggressively. Never allow the raging storm to deafen you to the voice of God. Please crossover to this powerful truth, nothing silences the voice of God. It is your ears that need to be perpetually engaged.

4. **Seize the moment** - Peter asked permission to join Jesus on the water and it was granted. Peter was not alone in the boat, but he alone seized the moment. All the disciples had the same sight, but Peter tapped into an open door that was given by heaven. Please do not allow your company or environment to blind you from your divine moment. Failure to seize divine moments can alter an individual/your life forever. One seized divine moment can alter your life forever. Peter was never the same man. He grabbed the moment and had new knowledge. No other disciple could testify of walking on water. Look at his resume. Never allow the fear or silence of your peers to rob you of that which awaits you. Seize your moment and walk through the door.

5. **Step out** - Peter stepped out of the boat and walked on the water. He never experienced the miraculous until he forsook the familiar. There will be no walking on water if you remain in your boat of logic, the usual safety and confinement. In seizing the moment, he had to make a

critical decision. As a fisherman he knew walking on water is not logical- so he must go against logic. The boat was his natural secured place- he must forsake earthly security. The boat represented his place of familiarity- he must leave the place of comfort. Like Peter did, you who are reading now, need to step out by faith into the will of God. Peter stepped out of the boat into contrary winds and rough waters. Crossover into this truth; stop waiting on the tides to be calm to go after your miracle. The unfavourable situation does not eliminate but magnifies your miracle. Peter stepped out, not on the water but upon faith.

6. **Too near** - Peter began to sink and cried unto Jesus. Jesus stretched His hand and saved him. This tells you that Peter had reached near to Jesus. Crossover in this wise, you have come too far; reached too near to doubt/quit now. Peter was too near his destination to lose focus. As you go forward, you must maintain focus.

7. **Opportunity for worship** – Look when the other disciples worshipped Jesus. Happy that they did, but only Peter seized the greater worship moment. When Jesus told Peter to come, and he stepped out of the boat that is deep level worship. That is not worship through singing, clapping, or dancing but worship of faith and

confidence. You are reading right now, and this is an instruction to you; elevate your worship. You have sung enough, now it is time to have faith and confidence in your God. The other disciples worshiped when the sea and storm had ceased– 'Good moment worshippers.' Peter worshipped amid fear and contrary winds. He worshipped when it was not the popular mode of expression. Crossover into new dimensions as you worship not because it is the popular thing, but because it is necessary.

SEIZE OPPORTUNITIES IN LACK

"And the third day there was a marriage in Cana of Galilee; and both Jesus was called, and His disciples, to the marriage. And when they wanted wine, the mother of Jesus saith unto Him, they have no wine. Jesus saith unto them, Fill the water pots with water. And they filled them up to the brim. And He saith unto them, Draw out now and bear unto the governor of the feast. And they bare it. When the ruler of the feast had tasted the water that was made to wine and knew not whence it was: (but the servants which drew the water knew) the governor of the feast called the bridegroom. And saith unto him, every man at the beginning doth set forth good wine; and when men have well drunk, then that which is worse: but thou hast kept the good wine until now." (St John 2:1-10).

What can we learn? Jesus did not panic at hearing of the lack. When you are in your winning season, you are super confident that Jesus has already made the way. Please note that He is not making the way, but rather revealing the already made way. Why did Mary tell Jesus? Did he bring wine with him? No. She revealed to him an opportunity. Jesus seized the moment. The lack was the opening Jesus seized to begin working miracles. According to John 2:11, *"This beginning of miracles did Jesus in Cana of Galilee and manifested forth his glory; and his disciples believed in him."*

Generating excellent results from lack transported his disciples to a cemented place of belief in him. Before there was a lack of wine, Jesus was not known as a miracle worker. Lack caused him to be exposed to those who were around him and beyond. We have not seen the wealth of lack because we are blinded to its potential. As you proceed in your daily exploits, fail no more to reap lack for all its hidden treasures. After the lack, they experienced the best-tasting wine ever. Hear this - this lack you are experiencing is a setup to have you walk through the best season of your life.

After the lack, you step into your best. Let us be bold and say, "From lack to best." Therefore, crossover into this new level of thanksgiving, and thank God for your lack. The days of lack will not last forever. This is it - your winning season. However, it is true that you should not use one account to derive a dogma. So, let's look again. *"Now there cried a certain woman of the wives of the sons of the prophets unto Elisha, saying, Thy servant my husband is dead, and thou knowest that thy servant did fear the LORD: and the creditor is come to take unto him my two sons to be bondmen. And Elisha said unto her, what shall I do for thee? Tell me, what hast thou in the house? And she said, thine handmaid hath not anything in the house, save a pot of oil. Then he said, go, borrow thee vessels abroad of all thy neighbours, even empty vessels; borrow not a few. And when thou art come in, thou shalt shut the door upon thee and upon thy sons, and shall pour out into all those vessels, and thou shalt set aside that which is full. So she went from him, and shut the door upon her and upon her sons, who brought the vessels to her; and she poured out. And it came to pass, when the vessels were full, that she said unto her son, Bring me yet a vessel. And he said unto her, there is not a vessel more. And the oil stayed. Then she came and told the man of God. And he said, Go, sell the oil, and pay thy debt, and live thou and thy children of the rest."* (2 Kings 4:1- 7)

I sincerely believe this widow did well. She married a man of God who was a prophet. Please do not be misinformed, true children of God experience challenges also. The challenges you now face is directly orchestrated to you saying at a deeper level, yes Lord yes! There are different levels of yes. From what level of yes have you responded?

The man of God had a problem and died without fixing it. He died leaving it to his wife. You must understand, the wealth of the marriage is shared, and so is the poverty. It's not just for the better. If that is the truth, why do so many others think of leaving a relationship because things are rough? Weak is the person who flees because the sea gets rough.

I admire this widow. She did not abandon her husband because he was not handling his finances efficiently; she stayed with him. You love him/her when they are prophesying, preaching, and doing the miracles but when the bills cannot be paid, you withhold sex and run. What about stickability?

She was husbandless and broke. The lack was such that she was about to lose her sons. She cried out in desperation. Watch this, if the husband had not died, she would not have spoken to the master prophet. His death opened the door for her to speak. Rather than cry out. She seized her winning season. Sometimes it takes death to unlock needed possibilities.

Her winning season was activated from the place of lack and desperation. If utilized wisely, lack is an activator. The senior prophet said to her, what do you have? May I ask you the same question, what do you have? Use it. The widow had in her house all this time, the door to her debt cancellation and living without financial distress; but she did not know.

Some people are like a bottle of oil, others see them but do not recognize their value. All along you are the door of breakthrough to the miraculous but they continue to live suffering because they underestimated you. After the provision was activated by the anointing upon the prophet's life, which served as the key, she poured and poured oil until all vessels were filled. From lack to abundance. In this winning season, you are going to experience a mighty shift from lack to abundance.

Please note there were three stages. Lack, preparation, and abundance. The preparation stage was getting the empty vessels. This was in anticipation of the move of God. What's your level of expectation? That will be made known by the number of vessels you gather. The magnitude of your preparation is a testimony of your faith and expectations. What level of preparation have you undertaken?

"Then she came and told the man of God. And he said, Go, sell the oil, and pay thy debt, and live thou and thy children of the rest." (2 Kings 4:7) 'The bed of debt is being burned right now.' That is a bed

you will not lay on again. The debtors already started making plans to seize your assets, but they will be disappointed. Your winning season is at hand. You will not lose anything or anyone in this season. She lost her husband and was about to lose her sons, but her seasons changed. No more loss. She was not only debt-free but also living comfortably. You will not have to wait for items to be on sale to be able to purchase. Credit cards paid off, school loan, mortgage, car loan- cleared in the name of Jesus Christ. I am celebrating with someone. I wish I knew your name. You are coming out of debt. Debt is becoming a soon-distant memory. Debt will become a testimony. Please declare, 'This is my winning season! My debts are cancelled, and I have enough to live comfortably.' You might have not seen it as yet but persistently declare and believe, "It is a done deal."

You are basking in your winning season. Nothing is impossible with God. Watch God work on your behalf. This is your season of testimonies.

CROSS OVER KEYS 🔑

1. This is your winning season.
2. A powerful necessary crossover truth is the storm is a key. It was designed to unlock the well-needed opportunity.

3. The contrary or opposition does not mean you are in the wrong or that you did not hear the voice of God.

4. Obstacles can easily be an indication that you are on the right path.

5. Never allow challenges faced to derail you from pursuing obedience to God.

6. The absence of change does not equate to the nonappearance of the presence of God.

7. Never allow the raging storm to deafen you to the voice of God.

8. Nothing silences the voice of God. It's our ears that need to be perpetually engaged.

9. Please don't allow your company or environment to blind you from your divine moment.

10. One ceased divine moment can alter your life forever.

11. There will be no walking on the water while you remain in your boat of logics, the usual, safety and confinement.

12. Stop waiting on the tides to be calm to go after your miracle. The un-favourable situations do not eliminate but magnifies your miracle.

13. You have come too far, reached too near to doubt/quit now.

CHAPTER SEVEN
WHEN GOD REQUEST A HARD THING

As you crossover into greater dimensions of thinking and being, you must grasp this not-so-pleasant truth - God will make some hard requests of you. The truth is, you would prefer if the requests from God were all easy, a walk in the park but the reality is, there are times when God's requests are hard and challenging. You rejoice as you recognize and embrace that this is your winning season. However, be cognizant that in this winning season, God might just make a hard request of you. We saw this in the life of Abraham.

"Now the LORD had said unto Abram, Get thee out of thy country, and from thy kindred, and from thy father's house, unto a land that I will shew thee: And I will make of thee a great nation, and I will bless thee, and make thy name great; and thou shalt be a blessing: And I will bless them that bless thee, and curse him that curseth thee: and in thee shall all families of the earth be blessed." (Genesis 12:1-3)

Abram was asked a hard thing. To leave behind all that he knew: his country, his kindred, and His father's household. It is like God said, I am rooting you up from where you are planted to replant you somewhere you know not. A simple truth is, God might want the same with you. Will you say yes to being replanted by God? Your winning season will be known by your replanting. Abram's winning season commenced with a hard request from God. In that hard request was embedded his turnaround and prosperity. For Abram, his uprooting was geographical but please know that physical location is not the only place of replanting. Other necessary areas are finances, emotions, spiritual, and relational. Cross over in this wise, the greatest of poverty is remaining where God has instructed you to leave.

Failure to obey God will see the soil of that area rejecting you. The soil will partner with God even when you refuse to. By God's request to Abram, the land of Terah where he abode, would no longer be favourable to him, it is compelled to cease being kind to him. The flip side to this is, you can be prosperous in a place but be living in disobedience. Prosperity does not equate to obedience. God again asked a hard thing from Abraham.

"And it came to pass after these things that God did tempt Abraham, and said unto him, Abraham: and he said, Behold, here I am. And he said, Take now thy son, thine only son Isaac, whom thou lovest, and get thee into the land of Moriah; and offer him there for a burnt offering upon one of the mountains which I will tell thee of." (Genesis 22:1-2)

God required all - His only son, whom he loved. That was a hard request. We sing I surrender all, but does that include everything? Does it include your children, resources, present and future? Are we sure about giving God our all? Lest you think God's hard requests were reserved for Abraham, let us look at the New Testament.

"Now the birth of Jesus Christ was on this wise: When as His mother Mary was espoused to Joseph before they came together, she was found with child of the Holy Ghost. Then Joseph her husband, being a just man, and not willing to make her a public example, was minded to put her away privily. But while he thought on these things, behold, the angel of the LORD appeared unto him in a dream, saying, Joseph, thou son of David, fear not to take unto thee Mary thy wife: for that which is conceived in her is of the Holy Ghost." (Matthew 1:18-20)

God asked Joseph to care for a child and to take Mary who was pregnant, of which he was not the one that impregnated her, to be his wife. I imagine myself in Joseph's position thinking, "Like seriously God! I have been waiting to have her as my wife. My virgin wife. And now she is pregnant! I will be the laugh of the town. She cheated. I cannot take her!" Then Joseph married her and never had sex with her until after the baby was born. What did he do wrong? But Joseph, like Abraham, obeyed.

The hard requests of loving those who have done you wrong can become overbearing. Loving your ex who cheated, abandoned you when he found out you were pregnant, or that friend who raped you, or even your parent who chose a partner over you.

A dear friend of mine, Chaneika was told by God to resign from her job. This meant one less income and then shortly after the family expanded. Yet she obeyed God and did as He requested. Will you be obedient to God when He asks that hard thing? Chaneika was earning more than her husband did. Does that make sense God? Why take away any of their income? And if you are going to take one, why not the lesser one? These are very serious questions. Please crossover into this truth - the more He takes from you, the greater He returns. Whenever God asks the hard things, He is building a deeper relationship with you. Reader let me reiterate, I wish I could tell you that serving and obeying God will always be easy, but it is not. However, it is worth it.

CROSS OVER KEYS

1. You must grasp this not-so-pleasant truth - God will make some hard requests from you.
2. Your winning season will be known by you being uprooted and replanted.

3. For Abram, his uprooting was geographical but please know that physical location is not the only place of replanting.

4. Cross over in this wise, the greatest of poverty is remaining where the soil has evicted you.

5. You can be prosperous in a place but be living in disobedience.

6. Prosperity does not equate to obedience.

7. Will you be obedient to God when He asks that hard thing?

8. The more God takes from you, the greater He returns.

CHAPTER EIGHT
HEAVEN'S CHOICE

In 1 Samuel chapter 16, we read the account of Samuel being instructed by God to anoint one of Jesse's sons as King, but David the youngest was not initially invited. After God rejected all the other sons, David was sent for. Verse 13 says, *"Then Samuel took the horn of oil, and anointed him in the midst of his brethren: and the Spirit of the LORD came upon David from that day forward."*

An awesome consecrated service took place. The uncalled son, David, was anointed in the presence of his father and brethren. You have been sidelined, overlooked; not considered worthy, but in this season, like David, heaven is going to point you out. The fact they overlooked you, might just be a sign that you are God's choice. The purpose of their act of overlooking you was to ensure God received all the glory when He, God establishes you. Hear this, your selection will not be based on your parent's good name, economic status, or educational achievements but solely on this - you are Heaven's choice. For years you have been faithful, served as you are led or asked to, but you have been sidelined and overlooked. The promotion that you wanted was taken and given to someone less deserving. You have cried to God about not being recognized for the hard work you have put in. Seems like everyone comes and takes you for a ride, but they do not see you. Hear what the Lord says, it was not that they did not see you, but rather He hid you for this season. God is about to remove the scales from the eyes of those whom He intends to partner with you. You are coming into your winning season and will not need everyone to see you, but only those who are assigned to help you. You will not need to force your way to your victory, ask someone to do you a favor or even pray about it anymore.

To substantiate this point let us look at the account of the colt found in Matthew 21:1-5. Jesus sent his disciples to fetch a colt that was never sat on. Mark's account puts it this way:

"And saith unto them, go your way into the village over against you: and as soon as ye be entered into it, ye shall find a colt tied, whereon never man sat; loose him, and bring him." (Mark 11:2)

Please do not ignore this information, no man has ever sat on the colt. No man saw the use of the colt. That is because he was being preserved to carry the Messiah. He was preserved. You are being preserved until your appointed time. Your time to be used by God is now. They could not see you because preserved mode was activated. This season will mess up your regular life's routine. Jesus rode into town on the colt. Hear this, the people threw their clothes on the ground. Who walked on the clothes, Jesus, or the donkey? It was the donkey. As you are sent for by the Holy Spirit, and you do the work of God, as persons honor God, they will not be able to avoid blessing you.

Let us use the colt and donkey to illustrate some powerful truths. Can you imagine how many times the colt was upset because they rode its mother and not it? Watching others being used but not him? But when his time came, he received honour that the others did not. No other can testify of walking on a person's clothing. Cross over with this truth, as you are revealed, you will surpass those who have gone before you. Your favour will usher you into speed mode. Do not be stressed about those who went on before you, support them. Your 'sent for a moment' is at hand; this is your season. your winning season.

Do not miss this, Jesus knew where the colt was; He told the disciples where to find the colt. All they had to do was obey and follow directives. Please commence thanking God now. Lord, we thank you for those who are sent for us, who will be in obedience and follow the directives of the Holy Spirit. We shut down their inclination to disobey. Thank you, Lord, for locating me. Rejoice, Jesus knows where you are. God is about to reveal who you are to some key persons. Recently a daughter of mine went to a job interview. During the session, the interviewer said, "The Holy Spirit just told me you need this breakthrough. I don't know how I am going to get you in the company, but I will have to figure it out".

Let the crossover continue with you believing. Look in the mirror, point to the person looking at you, and say, you are heaven's choice. Repeat it until you truly believe it. TD Jakes in one of his sermons said, that some Bible scholars believe that David shed some light on why he was not called to this anointing service in Psalms 51, behold, I was brought forth in iniquity, and in sin did my mother conceive me. He said it suggested that he was an illegitimate child.

As you pursue crossing over from low thinking to a higher dimension of processing, please embrace this - nothing about your past is powerful enough to override the plans of God for your life - no abortions, divorce, murder, same-sex relationships, time in prison, children out of wedlock, etc. Hear this truth; God saw you when no one else knew or recognized you. That is the beauty of God's favour. Like David, the fulfilment of the meeting will not be accomplished until you are invited and anointed. Without that happening. Heaven will not allow another to take your place. For all who have been having some near misses; you see, and smell, but have not been able to grasp that which you desire. In this season, you will not be denied anymore. This is your time. God has seen your faithfulness in private and is about to reward you publicly. The anointing for appointment will distinguish you as heaven's choice. The anointing of God speaks unapologetically for you.

Samuel saw the eldest son and said, "Yes, this is surely the one," but God said no, this is not the one. Please understand that God has sent back persons to pray again; because until they have come to the place of accepting what Heaven is saying about you, they will have to continue. Samuel went through all who were presented, but none was heaven's choice. Samuel could not rest until Heaven's choice, David, was brought forth. Cross over with this humble truth; there are leaders, families, and nations who are waiting on you so they can rest.

Normally, the door would be shut, but because you are in your winning season, Heaven will speak on your behalf and the supposed closed door will be flung wide open. No more shut doors in Jesus' name. This season has nothing to do with your qualifications, or the recommendations from your pastor or former employer. No. Please understand, that this is all God.

Like the colt who had no experience, no resume or recommendation from previous employers but was sent for, God will send for you. You are entering a season that is unfamiliar to you, with no experience or reference points to guide you. Please hear this: when you are in the public domain and God is astonishing you, maintain your composure. When you get home, fall to the ground and worship God. This is the season you have been waiting for.

Some of David's brothers were trained soldiers in military warfare in the army of Saul. The unrecognized David was also trained in warfare but by God. As you cross over, do not be stressed about the training of others, master your training. An excellent question to ask as you consider a relationship, or a position is, who trained you?

David received his anointing and trouble brewed in the place where his anointing would take him. There was calm, and peace... until you were anointed. God held back the crisis until you were anointed to handle it. The situations that are being manifested now, are because you are positioned and anointed to handle them. You are heaven's choice to deal with this matter. Pastor Alph Lukau said it like this, "I did not improvise myself, God anointed me for difficult matters." We see this sentiment being taught in Exodus 18:17-22, *"Jethro said to Moses, the thing you are doing is not good. You are wearing yourself out. Appoint leaders to administer over the affairs. The hard matters they take to you."* This is it; you are preserved for the hard matters. You are anointed to deal with hard matters, you must understand your anointing; not every battle is yours to fight. Some battles are below your anointing. That might sound arrogant, but it is true. You will never see the commissioner of police doing spot checks; it is below his assignment. Please function where your anointing has positioned you. Never underestimate your training. Like David, you are not approved to be victorious in the physical domain only but also in the spiritual.

There is a difference between talent and anointing; do not miss it. The evil spirit troubled Saul and David was called to play music. David's talent was his ability to play the harp, but it was the anointing in his life that fueled his talent and drove the evil spirit away. What are you operating through - talent or anointing? Talent alone is entertainment; the anointing makes it an effective ministry. While your gifts and calling make room for you, it will take the anointing and submission to the Holy Spirit to maintain where you have been called to.

Please pay close attention to the words of 1 Samuel 16:18; *"Then answered one of the servants, and said, Behold, I have seen a son of Jesse the Bethlehemite, that is cunning in playing, and a mighty valiant man, and a man of war, and prudent in matters, and a comely person, and the LORD is with him"*.

Hear Saul's servant, David is a man of war.... Wait, he is not in the army, how is he known to be a man of war? Someone needs to get this quickly. You were not allowed to function in the public domain, but where you were/are, in the place of private wilderness, God allows persons to acknowledge you and to be aware of what you carry. What God has deposited in you, no matter where you are, will be known. Serve where you are, knowing that, when the time is right, God will usher you into your place of influence. Look, David did not apply for the position, the position was presented to him. There are instances where you will need to apply, but do not be afraid to cross over to this truth - because you are Heaven's choice, you will not need to apply for the next big move, you will be sent for.

Now watch the transition of the anointing. David moved from feeding sheep to standing before the king in the palace. I hear this question; can you handle the anointing? Please do a link, the army of Israel had a crisis to which Saul the King had no solution; however, David was sent to his brethren and intervened in the matter. Two major points in David's life came from a crisis; one was Saul's problem, and the other was a national one. Never underestimate the power and abundance embedded in a crisis. Please, grasp this cross-over necessity; you are not just anointed to handle individual issues, there is the national and international CRISIS anointing on you. Never believe that helping Saul (an individual) is the pinnacle of your ministry, nations are waiting. As you do one on one ministry, pay close attention to the caliber or ranking of those you help, it is an indicator of the wider ministry.

Now watch this, God knew David, and where he was. God knew the plans He had for him. David was merely being preserved until the hard matters were at hand; that is why you have been overlooked. Listen, do not play with your anointing. I remember I was entertaining junk (things that were not pleasing to God) and the Lord used me mightily one day to bring forth someone's deliverance. When He was through, He said, this is what you are playing with.

The anointed David enquired about the war and was met with disdain. Readers do not be fooled, the anointing exposes your haters, so do not be mad at them. Do not apologize for your anointing, anyone who has a problem with it, let them take it up with God. It was the custom to bestow a peculiar blessing on the eldest son, Abinadab was the first and David the last. God wants someone to understand that Heaven is not bound to the custom of men. Heaven does not have to fit into the system of men, being the last has positioned you to be first. Reject the invite to be bombarded with jealousy towards those who are before you. God is moving persons from last to first, this is the turning point in your life. Cross over with this transformation - you are heaven's choice.

As the Lord ushers you into your winning season, please understand, that you will have to do things differently. The time of tears, of sorrow, must now be replaced with jubilation of praise and worship. Gladness must demonstrate a shift in attitude. Where forgiveness was lacking, you must now promote quick forgiveness. The seat of believing something is too good for you must be abandoned. In this your winning season, remove the limitations you have placed on God, and now increase your level of expectations. You must believe and expect that God will do it, rather He has done it. Wear the attitude of praise and thanksgiving. You stopped rejoicing because you did not see the manifestation of that which you desired happen on your timing but now rejoice again.

You need to increase your faith; hence, increase your expectations. In the dry season, you asked for small and expected small. In this winning season, increase your asking by millions of times with matching expectations. As you ask, so shall you receive. There are some projects that you started and stopped, this is the season to restart and bring to completion.

This is where even the errors you make are corrected by God. Yes, you did blunder and were positioned to fail, but God is making your crooked paths straight. In this season, you must worship where others are worried or depressed. They wonder if you are crazy. In this season, favours, miracles, and blessings will search for you, they will locate you. No matter how the enemy tries to hide you, you will be found. Notice, you will not be the one searching for favours, but rather, favour will pursue you.

Samuel left and went in search of Heaven's choice. Do you know that the blessings of the Lord that are searching for you, will cause men to wait on you? It will cause you to be sent for; not recognized but sent for. In your winning season, persons who are recommended will be rejected to make way for you. This is where their recommendations are invalid. There is a major difference between being recommended and being sent for. David did not take part in the sacrifice that Samuel made; do not be upset, the parade was not for you. You will arrive after the parade.

"And the LORD said, Arise, anoint him: for this is he." (1 Samuel 16:12b) Hear God speak on your behalf. Who is speaking on your behalf? God says, anoint him/her; this is the declaration for this season; anoint him/her. Heaven sanctions you. You

were not invited to the ceremony, but you are anointed in the presence of all those who paraded, not only them but those who had the authority to invite you to the ceremony and did not. It is like God gave you a grand entrance. The chosen you must be seen.

In your winning season, you might not be given an opportunity by the others to...but God will position or promote you before the detractors, the show cannot go on without you. All who said, they do not need you, will come to realize their folly. Your relevance will be made known in this season.

My sincere prayer for you, is God help you to remain humble as He blesses you in this season.

CROSS OVER KEYS

1. Hear this, your selection will not be based on your parent's good name, economic status, and educational achievements but solely on this - you are Heaven's choice.
2. The fact they overlooked you, is a sign that you are God's choice.
3. You are coming into your winning season and will not need everyone to see you, but only those who are assigned to help you.

4. You are being preserved until your appointed time.

5. Your favour will usher you into speed mode.

6. Let the cross-over continue with you believing.

7. As you pursue crossing over from low thinking to a higher dimension of processing, please embrace this - nothing about your past is powerful enough to override the plans of God for your life.

8. The anointing for appointment will distinguish you as heaven's choice.

9. You are anointed to deal with hard matters.

10. Serve where you are, knowing that, when the time is right, God will usher you into your place of influence.

11. In this your winning season, you might not get tickets for the show, but God has positioned you. The show cannot go on without you.

CHAPTER NINE

"FAST TRACK"

Fast track speaks to an acceleration of the development or progress of (a person or project). In the book of Jonah, we see a powerful account of fast track. Jonah was sent by Jehovah to preach to the city of Nineveh, but he disobeyed and pursued his desires. He did not want God to have mercy on the Ninevites. Jonah wanted them punished for their wickedness. Therefore, he took a ship to flee from the presence of God. His trip was interrupted by a storm, and he was thrown overboard. However, God spared his life by preparing a huge fish to swallow him. Jonah 2:10 and Jonah 3:3-4 write, respectively: *"And the LORD spake unto the fish, and it vomited out Jonah upon the dry land." "So, Jonah arose, and went unto Nineveh, according to the word of the LORD. Now Nineveh was an exceeding great city of three days' journey. And Jonah began to enter into the city a day's journey, and he cried, and said, yet forty days, and Nineveh shall be overthrown."*

Jonah received an assignment from God, and he decided to go against the will of God. What he did not understand was that because he was Heaven's choice, Heaven was going to assist him in completing the task. Cross over with this truth - every assignment given to you by God comes with a package. This package gives you all the support you need to complete the task. God did not give you a task and leave you alone. For Jonah, his package included a storm, being thrown overboard, and swallowed by a fish, experiencing hell, repentance, and realignment to the will of God, and then being vomited out; that was a heavy package.

The truth is that the package must match the assignment; the assignment was heavy, and a nation was on the brink of destruction. Your assignment is an indicator of your package. Having established that foundation, look at your own life. You now understand that all the hurts, disappointments, pain, rejection, lack, divorce, abortions, miscarriage, denied loans, etc., were a part of your package. I am not just saying this to sound deep; I have proven this to be true.

I went through a horrible marriage and suffered immensely; not knowing it was a part of my supporting package. Now I can minister to hurting husbands and wives from a place of empathy and sincerity. Going forward, when the bad comes upon you, just smile, and say, "Thank you God for this package." TD Jakes said it this way, "nothing you have been through shall be wasted." What I did not realize at the time was, the hurt was a training process. The pain you have been through shall not be wasted.

Not one lie told on you shall be wasted. Repeatedly you hear people saying that they do not know their purpose. Deep revelation of your purpose will be realized if you start looking at your package.

A journey that should have taken Jonah three days was completed within a day. Although he went into a ship that was going in the opposite direction, he arrived at the place of his assignment ahead of time. Jonah's assignment was fast-tracked. Many of you have been ushered into fast track because you have wasted much time, and the appointed time is drawing near. The assignment that has been entrusted to you requires heaven's assistance therefore you are now placed on the fast track. This is where you will see miraculous divine connections. You are not assigned to fail; people are waiting for your arrival. Their future resides in your arrival and obedience.

I will not tell you it is easy however, speaking from a renewed mind and the assurance given to the saints according to Romans 8:28, you know even the not so easy is all going to work out for your good. A good observation is Jonah's package was because of his disobedience. However, if we remember the three Hebrew boys of Daniel Chapter 3, they were determined to obey God and were thrown into a fire that was increased seven times. The fire was a part of their package which ended in them being fast tracked to a promotion in Babylon. Whether or not you started in disobedience or obedience, the assignment must be completed, and it will come with challenges.

"WHERE ARE YOU?"

Where are you is a frequent question that is echoed daily as persons seek to ascertain the location of those they need to be in contact with. God asked the same question in Genesis 3:8-9: *"And they heard the voice of the LORD God walking in the garden in the cool of the day: and Adam and his wife hid themselves from the presence of the LORD God amongst the trees of the garden. And the LORD God called unto Adam, and said unto him, where art thou?"*

God asked Adam, where art thou? Does this question suggest that God was not aware of where Adam was? If yes, that would mean God is not all-knowing. Therefore, that is not the essence.

God intended to reveal to Adam that though geographically he was in the garden, spiritually he was not at the place he was the last time they met. The spiritual connection between them had been broken.

This reality is a true possibility for you today. This happens when we are geographically present at church, prayer meeting, and Bible study, but have lost our connection with God. Watch this, Adam and Eve did not hide until they heard the voice of God. This is where many persons are; at a place of separation from God but continue to show up and serve until they are exposed by God.

Look at this, *"Now there was a day when the sons of God came to present themselves before the LORD, and Satan came also among them."* (Job 1:6) Satan was separated but continued to show up. Do not believe that because you show up it means you are in right standing with God. Cross over in this wise, being present does not equate to right standing.

Look at John 13:26-27 *"Jesus answered, He it is, to whom I shall give a sop when I have dipped it. And when he had dipped the sop, he gave it to Judas Iscariot, the son of Simon. And after they sop Satan entered him. Then said Jesus unto him, what thou doest, do quickly."*

Here was the final meeting with Jesus and all His disciples before his crucifixion. Who was there? Satan. Question, are you present where you are supposed to be? Is Satan present and you are absent? Where are you?

The question asked by God to Adam was directly related not to his physical but his spiritual position. What is the condition of your Spirit? Are you right with God? It is futile to pretend. If you are in a broken state with God, get it mended. This is the truth, no amount of sacrifice, tithes and offerings, singing, praying, giving to the poor, prophesying, etc. can erase a broken relationship. If your heart is not in cohesion with the Spirit of God, you are out of order.

Look at this, Adam hid from God, but Satan had conversations with God. This is serious.

Think about this... while you are finding it a struggle to pray because of the situations you are going through, Satan is engaging God against you? He is accusing you while you are silent with God. Are you silent because you are entangled in the midst of the confusion? Are you a part of the problem? Job chapter one shines some light on the magnitude of your location.

"Then Satan answered the LORD, and said, doth Job fear God for nought? Hast not thou made a hedge about him, and about his house, and about all that he hath on every side? Thou hast blessed the work of his hands, and his substance is increased in the land." (Job 1:9-10)

Pay attention, Satan had information on Job. What information does Satan have on you? Does he know where you are? What have you given Satan to be used in his case against you?

Recently I saw the following, "you cannot rebuke the demon you are sleeping with". Please look at Jonah.

Jonah was sent to Nineveh but chose to go to Tarshish. Here is something to ponder: Are you where God instructs you to be? Where are you? Does where you are carry the mark of obedience? God is not impressed with your fancy dressing or eloquent speeches. He is looking at your heart. Where your heart is, and what is its condition? Are you promoting the Kingdom of God or your own agenda?

Whenever you are not where God has ordained you to be, it is a form of robbing God. Predominantly when we talk about robbing God we go to the following -Malachi 3:8, "Will a man rob God? Yet ye have robbed me. But ye say, wherein have we robbed thee? In tithes and offerings?" I submit to you, robbing God is not limited to just tithes and offering. Look at robbery: according to the Oxford online Dictionary, robbery is the action of taking property unlawfully from a person or place by force or threat of force. When someone is robbed, they are deprived of what is rightfully theirs. 1 Corinthians 14:39 intimated that, when the Holy Spirit gives you a word for your friend, church, nation, and you withhold it, you are robbing God and the people. "Wherefore, brethren, covet to prophesy, and forbid not to speak with tongues." Jonah tried to rob God of expressing His

116

compassion to Nineveh and the people from hearing the expressed mind of God. Where are the ones who are willing to be ridiculed, ostracized, and banished for the Lord's sake? It is time for the prophets to stop curtailing the word of God to please the people. If God gives you a word of rebuke, do not 'cook it over' and share a word of peace. Who told you and you believed that you should not speak in tongues? If you refuse to speak in tongues, you are robbing God and yourself of spiritual communication. This truth is substantiated by the words of Paul in 1 Corinthians 14:2, 4 which reads; *"For he that speaketh in an unknown tongue speaketh not unto men, but unto God: for no man understandeth him; howbeit in the spirit he speaketh mysteries. He that speaketh in an unknown tongue edifieth himself."*

PLACE OF WILLINGNESS?

The word of God says if you refuse to forgive, you will not be forgiven. This means God wants to forgive you but if you do not forgive, He is robbed of this opportunity to bless you. You might question if God's sovereign will is conditional on the will of another. Please allow me to use the words of St. John 3:16 to respond. It is God's sovereign will that every man be saved, however, salvation received by anyone depends upon the action (acceptance of that person).

You are exhorted according to 1 Thessalonians 5:18, in this wise, *"In everything give thanks: for this is the will of God in Christ Jesus concerning you."* You see a mighty display of this grace in the account of Paul and Silas; after being beaten and thrown in prison they demonstrated this for you.

Acts 16:25 reads; *"And at midnight Paul and Silas prayed and sang praises unto God: and the prisoners heard them. Suddenly there was a great earthquake so that the foundations of the prison were shaken: and immediately all the doors were opened, and everyone's bands were loosed".*

You rob God when you allow rough situations to take away your worship. Yes, it is true. You lock the possibilities of heaven. God wants to demonstrate that He is magnificent on the earth, but you have been robbing Him of opportunities. I love the expressed heart and location of Mary the mother of Jesus according to the book of Luke.

"And the angel said unto her, Fear not, Mary: for thou hast found favour with God. And behold, thou shalt conceive in thy womb, and bring forth a son, and shalt call his name JESUS... Then said Mary unto the angel, how shall this be, seeing I know not a man? And the angel answered and said unto her, The Holy Ghost shall come upon thee, and the power of the Highest shall overshadow thee: therefore also that holy thing which shall be born of thee shall be called the Son

of God... And Mary said, Behold the handmaid of the Lord; be it unto me according to thy word. And the angel departed from her." (Luke 1:30, 31, 34, 35, 38)

Mary's response tells you where she was – 'be it unto me according to thy words'. She was located at a place that did not require her to negotiate, argue, or make excuses. Her address was the epiphany of willingness. Please cross over with this truth - your response testifies about you. Pay attention to a person's response. The prophet Isaiah's response to God also revealed he was located at willingness. Isaiah 6:8 says: *"Also I heard the voice of the Lord, saying, whom shall I send, and who will go for us? Then said I, here am I; send me."*

Are you at the place of willingness? How long now has the Holy Spirit been trying to get you to move? Who is suffering because you have been refusing to obey the instructions of God and preventing the activation of the anointing because you are not at the place of your calling?

Care must be taken to ensure that you are divinely located. Pay attention to your address commencing with obedience.

CROSS OVER KEYS

1. Every assignment given to you by God comes with a package.

2. The truth is that the package must match the assignment.

3. Your package is an indicator of your assignment.

4. The pain you have been through shall not be wasted.

5. Whether in disobedience or obedience, the assignment must be completed, and it will come with challenges.

6. Let us not believe that because we show up it means we are in right standing with God. Cross over in this wise, being present does not equate to right standing.

7. If your heart is not in cohesion with the Spirit of God, you're in trouble.

8. You rob God when you allow rough situations to take away your worship.

9. Please cross over with this truth - your response testifies about you.

10. It is imperative that care be taken to ensure that you are divinely located. Pay attention to your address commencing with obedience.

CHAPTER TEN
DISAPPOINTED INTO YOUR
APPOINTMENT

Being the recipient of disappointments is never easily welcomed. Your expectations are shattered, and a different reality is manifested. But in the disguise of pain, disappointment can indeed be the channel used to usher you into your appointment. The book of Ruth will be used to establish this truth.

"So, they two went until they came to Bethlehem. And it came to pass, when they were come to Bethlehem, that all the city was moved about them, and they said, Is this Naomi? And she said unto them, call me not Naomi, call me Mara: for the Almighty hath dealt very bitterly with me. I went out full, and the LORD hath brought me home again empty: why then call ye me Naomi, seeing the LORD hath testified against me, and the Almighty hath afflicted me? So, Naomi returned, and Ruth the Moabitess, her daughter in law, with her, which returned out of the country of Moab: and they came to Bethlehem in the beginning of barley harvest." (Ruth 1:19- 22)

Naomi and Ruth left Moab and arrived in Bethlehem Judah. The writer did not merely include that it was harvest time because space needed to be filled, but that bit of information is critical.

121

In the book *Mind Renewal: Biblical Secrets to a Better You*, this scripture was used to teach timing and motives, now it is used to highlight seasons. Every season comes with different levels of demands, expectations, and rewards. Knowing the season that you have crossed over into prepares and positions you to be ready for what that season requires and must give. The more fruitful the season will be, the greater your input is expected.

In Ruth 2:2 Ruth asked her mother-in-law to allow her to go and glean in the field belonging to Boaz. This she did because it was harvesting time; she knew it was not planting time. Please be careful to heed what the season requires. You have suffered a long period but when you make that one shift, you will be realigned into the favour of God. The shift Naomi and Ruth made was a geographical one. Yours might be crossing over from your percentage of consumption.

The truth is, we have been consuming our tomorrow as we fail to invest for the future. How is your salary divided? What percentage goes to consumption, savings, and investments? As you cross over, please relocate from no, or low investment, to solid future securing deposits. Reassign a portion of the consumption sum to investments. The new season requires you to think and act differently. Do not go into your new season with the old season's method of thinking.

Naomi returned to the place where she left because of famine, lack, and not enough, but returned just in time for abundance. Things will not always remain the same. The last time Naomi was in Bethlehem, she experienced scarcity, but now she is experiencing harvest time. God will send you back to the place of your former suffering and bless you in the presence of those who knew your pain. The famine is no more, sickness disappeared, and empty accounts are filled.

Cross-over into this revolution - God has prepared for you a different experience. You have cried out but now wipe your tears. You might still feel like you want to cry but speak to yourself in this wise, "tears of pain your time has expired, it is my rejoicing time". Please embrace this truth, tears have an expiration date, and that is now. Wait, wait, wait... not just tears but sadness, depression, lack, almost, sickness, loneliness, etc., and it is now.

Naomi was so torn by her experiences that she decided to have a name change. She said do not call me Naomi, call me Mara. As you pursue cross-over, before you lie the following question, "Are you going to be detained by Mara (Bitterness) or rescued back to Naomi (Pleasantness)?

Within you resides the decision to be named Naomi or Mara. As you cross over, please rescue Naomi from out of Mara. The

123

truth is you are not Mara (bitter) you are Naomi (pleasant). Naomi, if you are not able to on your own, get help and reject abiding in Mara. The expiry date established on Mara is today. Now establish your faith in this wise. The present conditions smell, taste, and look bitter but you're going to live and demonstrate the pleasant dance, shout, worship, and thanksgiving. You have crossed over into a high dimension when you can rejoice in spite of. It is like springtime in winter. You embark on a Naomi worship although Mara is evident.

A major error that continues to plague many is not working the season. Look at Ruth, she jumped into a new role, she was in a new environment, but she adjusted her mind to the season. You must align your mind with your new season. This is a journey and not an event. Years ago, my season of poverty changed but my mind did not. I now had money to buy what I needed but still spent a good portion of my supermarket time checking the discount items and buying things I did not want, just because they were on sale. I was imprisoned for a season. Refuse the imprisonment of an expired season. Stop swimming in lack even though abundance is plenty.

Cross over into this truth – It is imperative that the people you are aligned or connected to, know their seasons. Ruth was connected to Naomi who understood her season of famine in

Bethlehem was over and that it is harvest time and guided her to Boaz's field. Boaz was prepared for her while she was a widow. She lost her husband to death which allowed her to remarry. Hear this powerful crossover truth - there are some disappointments that come so you can be appointed.

If Ruth had not suffered the pain, and agony of burying her late husband, she could not be positioned now for the wealthy, influential Boaz to marry her. Your pain is a key to unlocking some futuristic possibilities. Never underestimate the wealth of your pain. Death was the channel used to usher her into a desired reality. Always remember, there is a big picture to your pain. Please look at the account of the three Hebrew boys in Daniel 3:28-30:

"Then Nebuchadnezzar spake, and said, Blessed be the God of Shadrach, Meshach, and Abednego, who hath sent his angel, and delivered his servants that trusted in him, and have changed the king's word, and yielded their bodies, that they might not serve nor worship any god, except their own God. Therefore, I make a decree, that every people, nation, and language, which speaks anything amiss against the God of Shadrach, Meshach, and Abednego, shall be cut in pieces, and their houses shall be made a dunghill: because there is no other God that can deliver after this sort. Then the king promoted Shadrach, Meshach, and Abednego, in the province of Babylon."

The background to the account is that King Nebuchadnezzar created a golden calf and ordered everyone to bow down to it, with the decree that anyone who did not bow down would be thrown into a fiery furnace. Despite the threat of death, the three boys were so committed to their belief, that they chose death. This is where many potential victories are lost- the place of threat. Daily threats are being released: economic, emotional, spiritual, etc. In *Mind Renewal: Biblical Secrets to A Better You*, we see a powerful key "You do not have control over what is said or done to you, but you have power over your response". They chose their response-we are not bowing.

The King was so wrath, he ordered the fire to be increased seven times hotter. This was an intentional persuasive tactic, but they stood firm. Cross over with this knowledge - persuasion is a powerful tool used by the enemy. Resistance to the enemy's persuasion is a priceless victory. According to verse 22, *"Therefore because the king's commandment was urgent, and the furnace exceeding hot, the flames of the fire slew those men that took up Shadrach, Meshach, and Abednego."*

Please cross over to this truth; you are stronger than you think. Bishop Noel Jones preached a message where he said, "I am not built to break". The soldiers died from the heat coming from the fire and the Hebrew boys survived the fire. Persons have encountered far less than what you have survived, and they have crashed or drowned. The grace from God that has been extended to you is not the same testimony of others. If it had not been for the Lord on your side, the volcano, hurricane, and fire would have devoured you repeatedly. Your testimony is, 'but God!'

The earthly domain ordered its mighty soldiers to carry out an evil act against representatives of the heavenly realm and heaven prevailed. Hear this powerful truth - even if they had died in the fire, Nebuchadnezzar would still have lost. Cross over with this truth - however, the matter unfolds you win. As a child of the Kingdom of God, your success is guaranteed. Death can never be victorious over the children of God. Death for the saints of God is not a finality but rather a mode of transportation into eternal peace. Therefore, death can never win.

Please know this, you are not the only beneficiary of your resistance to the enemy. There are times when the enemy benefits also. Elevate your service to God so that your enemies reap well from your commitment. The King was exposed to revelatory knowledge which caused him to acknowledge and address the Hebrew boys' God as the only true and living God.

When you commit completely to God, regardless of the pressures of life, please know you will be vindicated. The same king, who ordered the boys thrown in the fire, turned around and ordered them to come out. This is where you cross over into a season of overrule. They expected the decree to be sustained but the King of all kings said it was overruled. Do not miss this truth; King Nebuchadnezzar was not the one who overruled the decree, it was the King of kings - Jesus. There is a powerful crossover key that we need not overlook.

Daniel chapter 3:27 reads as follows:

"And the princes, governors, and captains, and the king's counselors, being gathered together, saw these men, upon whose bodies the fire had no power, nor was the hair of their head singed, neither were their coats changed, nor the smell of fire had passed on them."

This was said earlier but let me reiterate. There is wealth and power in your pain! The king made a decree which exposed the hidden big picture of the Hebrew boys' ordeal. He said, *"Therefore I make a decree, that every people, nation, and language, which speak anything amiss against the God of Shadrach, Meshach, and Abednego, shall be cut in pieces, and their houses shall be made a dunghill: because there is no other God that can deliver after this sort."* (Daniel 3:29)

It is not your prerogative to know or comprehend how God will do it. But as you unreservedly commit to God, your enemies will have no choice but to acknowledge Him. Truth is, it was never about you. God must be glorified.

But before we return to Ruth, let's look at verse 30 of Daniel 3, *"Then the king promoted Shadrach, Meshach, and Abednego, in the province of Babylon."*

Please understand that the promotion came after the persecution. Every dimension of elevation comes with testimonies of pressure. No pressure, no valuable elevation. My brother Stokely once told me, "Pressure busts pipes or sends water uphill." How do you respond to pressure? Will you be relocated as you are promoted, or will you allow life's pressure to break you? Romans 8:18 says, *"For I reckon that the sufferings of this present time are not worthy to be compared with the glory which shall be revealed in us."* This all includes persecution and pressure. Is it remotely possible that the present crisis you are encountering is the master key to your well-deserved elevation through promotion? Like the Hebrew boys, Ruth's pain worked for her good.

Ruth tapped into a season of favour. She was seen by Boaz. This occurred because of her pursuit to serve her mother-in-law. May you tap into that grace where persons who are entrusted with the ability and gifts to move you from one dimension to another, see you. Do not go searching for a cavalry but rather, one person. Be so in-tuned to know who your appointed help is. In your search, you will need to leave behind certain seasons and their occupants.

LEAVE BEHIND

As you cross over into greater heights and deeper depths, please understand that there are things you love that you will need to leave at the cemetery. No joke. Many persons are depriving the cemetery of its tenants. Refuse to be a grave robber. Stop walking around with dead stuff - dead relationships, dead jobs, etc. Please learn from Ruth, she had to release Mahlon to embrace Boaz. Many persons are not married because they are not single. Physically single but spiritually, and mentally they are still in a relationship with someone who by now is married with children. This is a powerful cross-over prayer, Lord please open my understanding to the knowledge of the things and persons whose season in my life has come to an end.

Ruth was in a new season which required her to act differently. She went to glean, and favour was granted to her. May favour locate you today. Boaz instructed his workers to leave grains for her, making her work easier. As you move to a new place of thinking, expect the grace of God to shift you into a season of accomplishments at an easier pace. You will not always have to work extremely hard to yield favorable results.

Boaz commanded the men not to trouble her. In this season, may God inspire men and women to speak coverage, protection, and no interference to you. Do you understand that God has allowed persons of influence to be speaking about you on your behalf? Hear this; instructions of favour towards you have been released.

In Ruth's new season, she presented herself to Boaz. She obeyed the directives of Naomi, not Mara and she obeyed. Be careful whose advice you attend to. Same person but who is speaking, Mara or Naomi? Truth is, not every piece of advice comes from Naomi, some are fuelled by Mara. Mara is bitter, hurting, and will want you to be bitter. This is where you are advised from a place of hurt/ an unhealthy place. While you appreciate advice, please evaluate the bed from which it rises. One bitter advice has the potential to destroy a nation. Ruth stepped out of the norm and went into Boaz. By doing so, she made her intentions known. Cross over into this truth - the days of passiveness are over. What norm must you vacate in this new season? Pursue with godly due diligence your desired future. Please pause and pray this prayer, "God, please cause the right person to see me". Boaz was a kinsman; he by tradition could redeem her. The right pair of eyes saw.

Ruth. You applied for jobs upon jobs, but no favourable response. Is it remotely possible that God has blinded their eyes to navigate you to His best for you? Lest you limit it to jobs, what about husbands, opportunities, etc.? Please cross over to this end; In the name of Jesus, we command every tired, lazy, bad-minded destiny helper to rise now. Get busy. Boaz went into another gear; he needed to put things in place, he was her destiny helper. In this new season, negotiations are being made on your behalf without you being present. Even when you are unaware, deals are being made in your favour. Boaz met with the elders of the town and negotiated for Ruth. Watch this, Ruth was married but was childless, she remarried and gave birth.

In this new season, you will produce where you previously failed. She would have lived and died thinking that she was barren, but God sent her Boaz with the key to the secret compartment. Grasp this, not everyone can open all your doors, some doors are reserved for divine connection. Never allow someone who has access to two doors to cause you to believe that all you have are two doors. Boaz brought out of Ruth what Mahlon failed to tap into. This does not mean Mahlon was bad or had a deficiency, but he did not carry the grace to unlock such glorious possibilities. Mahlon ran from famine and married Ruth; Ruth ran from idolatry, a place of painful memories, and married Boaz. Which direction are you running? Be careful who you allow to be attached to you. Find out where they are running from and from what. Remember in Jonah chapter 1, Jonah ran from God and caused chaos on the mariners.

Increase your level of thinking to this possibility - your current place of employment is more than your job; it is your investment. Ruth tapped into a season where she became part owner of the place she once gleaned. Hear this; the bakery you work at now can be yours. As you cross over into this grace, your elevation will happen swiftly. The same persons who you sought favour from, will now seek favour from you. Be careful how you treat those who are seemingly in a lesser altitude than you are. Changes can be sudden, the last becomes the first swiftly.

As your season changes, you must fit into your role. You cannot be promoted to wife/husband and still want to glean. It is not that you are better than gleaning, but your season comes with promotion.

Change your garment, do your hair, put on good perfume, and ride on the chariot beside your Boaz with your baby Obed. This might be challenging for some to embrace because of the duration of their gleaning. But please cross over with your season into this beauty-gleaning days are over. Ruth 4:13 says, *"So Boaz took Ruth, and she was his wife: and when he went in unto her, the LORD gave her conception, and she bare a son."* Ruth was transported from being a gleaner to a wife. Her entire life changed. The account of Ruth is used but let us not fail to see the gender-neutral truth in the elevation. This is available to both males and females.

No delay. The Lord gave her conception. Wait, look again. The Lord gave her conception. God opened the door for Boaz. Lest you think it is your doing, just remember God helped you out. I love what Ruth did, look at Ruth 4:16-17: *"And Naomi took the child, and laid it in her bosom, and became nurse unto it. And the women her neighbours gave it a name, saying, there is a son born to Naomi, and they called his name Obed: he is the father of Jesse, the father of David."*

Ruth came into her new season and never forgot or turned a blind eye to Naomi. Never forget those who were loyal and struggled with you in your rough season. God wants you to be grateful however, never allow anyone to use their act of kindness to manipulate you. This is your season hence by no means apologize for the favour of God upon your life. Anyone that has an issue with your new season, refer them to God. It's His doing, not yours. Know your new season and walk into it. Rejoice, you deserve it.

CROSS OVER KEYS

1. Every season comes with different levels of demands, expectations, and rewards.
2. The more fruitful the season will be, the greater your input is expected.
3. The truth is that we have been consuming our tomorrow as we fail to invest in the future.
4. As you cross over, please relocate from no, or low investment, to solid future securing deposits.
5. Don't go into your new season with the old season's degree of thinking.
6. Every season comes with different levels of demands, expectations, and rewards.
7. The more fruitful the season will be, the greater your input is expected.
8. You have crossed over into a high dimension when you can rejoice despite.
9. Refuse the imprisonment of an expired season.
10. Some disappointments comes so you can be appointed.

11. It is important that you be careful of the people you are aligned or connected to and know their seasons.

12. Disappointed into your appointment.

13. Your pain is a key to unlocking some futuristic possibilities.

14. Persuasion is a powerful tool used by the enemy.

15. Resistance to the enemy's persuasion is a priceless victory.

16. Every dimension of elevation comes with testimonies of pressure.

CHAPTER ELEVEN
TOO MUCH TO GAIN TO LOSE

This is your winning season; you cannot afford to throw it away; you have waited too long. The tides have turned in your favour run with it, bask in it, and facilitate no distractions. Popular comedian Jim Carey's father lost his job as an accountant which saw the family plummet into poverty. Carey pursued his dreams of becoming a successful comedian but struggled greatly. One day he wrote himself ten years, post-dated cheque of ten million dollars with the words, for acting services rendered. Carey became an icon in Hollywood earning hundreds of millions. Carey saw beyond what the situation (poverty) at the time was shouting and envisioned himself earning millions for his work. He foresaw much to be gained and pursued not losing his vision. Like Carey, Blind Bartimaeus saw and pursued gaining that which could easily be lost.

"And they came to Jericho: and as he went out of Jericho with his disciples and a great number of people, blind Bartimaeus, the son of Timaeus, sat by the highway side begging. And when he heard that it was Jesus of Nazareth, he began to cry out, and say, Jesus, thou son of David, have mercy on me. And many charged him that he should hold his peace: but he cried the more a great deal, Thou son of David, have mercy on me. And Jesus stood still and commanded him to be called.

137

And they call the blind man, saying unto him, Be of good comfort,
rise; he calleth thee. And he, casting away his garment, rose, and came
to Jesus. And Jesus answered and said unto him, what wilt thou that
I should do unto thee? The blind man said unto him, Lord, that I might
receive my sight. And Jesus said unto him, Go thy way; thy faith hath
made thee whole. And immediately he received his sight, and followed
Jesus in the way." (Mark 10: 46-52)

To the masses, he was insignificant because of his condition and situation. His Condition- Blind Situation- Beggar. Crossover into this truth - your labelled misfortunes can be that which ushers you into the presence of God. The place of brokenness and misfortunes attracts the attention of God.

Please permit me to submit to you that Bartimaeus was not the only blind person in that huge crowd of people. Between verses 47 and 48 of Mark 10, those with physical eyesight failed to see what Bartimaeus saw. They were all blinded, just at different dimensions. Bartimaeus saw his opportunity to be healed, for his life to make a paradigm shift and he shouted, "Jesus thou son of David have mercy on me." He sought to get the attention of Jesus and the physically seeing, but spiritually blinded, told him to shut up; they failed to see what Bartimaeus saw. He was seeing at a level that they had not tapped into. His shouting was a form of worship unto God. He shouted from the dimension of - I must get my breakthrough. Please never allow anyone or the system to silence your shout- but not just your shout but your place of seeing. Your shout will be disdained because it is not understood. How can they understand when they are seeing from a low place? Lower than where you have tapped into?

Bartimaeus tapped into a realm called 'Closed mouth does not get fed.' He heard about a Power that could change his entire existence and became hungry with a mindset that if he perished, he perished, and decided to open his mouth by any means necessary. He was already blind, so he did not care who was looking or what they had to say, all he knew was his shout was for a needed change.

He was exposed to possibilities that the people telling him to shut up, did not need. Please, stop expecting people to understand your praise, dance, or shout; they do not have your need, nor have they received at the dimension from which you have received.

Always let your spiritual sight propel you to a place of desire that surpasses the well-meaning, yet negative utterances of those who are around you. The more they told him to be silent the more he shouted. Please adopt this, let your vision push you through the rubble of the crushers. Never cease.

The people saw the obvious in the physical but Bartimaeus through hearing of the saviour tapped into sight beyond sight. He saw possibilities and light and faith pushed him beyond where he was. His imagination somehow ignited him to keep on shouting. His shout, I believe, overpowered every other voice. His shout echoed a language that attracted the mercy he sought a language that is uttered from the chronicles of the physically impaired but spiritually alert.

Do not believe that all men are seeing from the same dimension. Amidst all the crowd of people, Jesus heard Bartimaeus. The blind beggar got the attention of Jesus. Question: what did Jesus hear and respond to? Was it Bartimaeus' voice or his needs? Please, decipher from where your words are being echoed voice or needs. I truly believe Jesus heard from the echo of needs and he responded in like manner.

The same people who were telling Bartimaeus to be silent were now given a job. Jesus said to bring him to come! Watch God turn the table around. You will be assisted by those who tried to crush you, God will change their assignment. They were not only charged to bring him before Jesus, but they had to make their way through the crowd. God will use those who previously tried to crush you, to make a way for you. They must secure a clear passage for you. Heaven has instructed them to ensure that you are not denied access anymore. Please do not resist when you see the change. This is God's doing.

According to verse 50, Bartimaeus cast off his garments before proceeding to Jesus. This was faith demonstrated at a high level. He determined that he would not need his beggars' garments after coming into communication with Jesus. He commenced living the freed life even before it was ordained upon him. He saw being healed before Jesus healed him. You must partner your works with your faith; demonstrate your faith through your works.

There is a bit of information that was left out about Bartimaeus by the writer. He was a wise man. He had two areas of need, sight, and money. Jesus asked what he, Bartimaeus, wanted and he responded, at the level of condition-recovery of sight. He understood that the situation is secondary to the condition which is primary. He was a beggar because he was blind and not blinded because he was a beggar. His response to Jesus showed that this wise man placed things in the right perspective. Crossover with this

wisdom - fix the primary and the secondary will fall in place. Jesus made it clear that he was aware of Bartimaeus' faith. He said, "Your faith has made you whole". We see Jesus expressing similar words to the woman with the issue of blood in Mark 5:34, "and he said unto her, daughter your faith has made you whole".

Are there any similarities between the two accounts? Yes, we see large crowds, conditions, situations, desperation, faith, and Jesus. Both Bartimaeus and the woman with the issue of blood demonstrated great levels of faith and received the same reward from Jesus. Have we missed what our faith can produce?

Faith serves as the currency that is used to complete the transaction of recovery. Sickness was confronted by faith and God was pleased. Being pleased He acted. Immediately Bartimaeus was healed. Persons are reading this book who are being ushered into a period of immediate. Things that you have desired, and hoped for are now yours immediately.

Bartimaeus now had sight and vision; he saw from the spiritual and the physical. The physical he used to navigate through earthly terrains, while the spiritual guided him to follow Jesus.

If you are seeing only from the physical domain, you are most dwarfed. Like Bartimaeus, please pursue sight through faith before sight from physical eyes.

CROSS OVER KEYS

1. Your labelled misfortunes can be that which ushers you into the presence of God.

2. Please never allow anyone or the system to silence your shout- but not just your shout but your place of seeing.

3. Please adopt this, let your vision push you through the rubble of the crushers. Never cease.

4. Always let your spiritual sight propel you to a place of desire that surpasses the well-meaning, yet negative utterances of those who are around you.

5. Please adopt this, let your vision push you through the rubble of the crushers.

6. You must partner your works with your faith.

7. Faith serves as the currency that is used to complete the transaction of recovery.

8. If you are seeing only from the physical domain, you are most dwarfed.

CHAPTER TWELVE
NECESSARY FRIENDSHIP

It is said if you have one good friend in a lifetime you are blessed. Friendship is something that we as humans desire. We are relational beings. Jesus taught us valuable lessons on friendship throughout his ministry. We will look at Judas and Peter.

We read in Matthew 16:21-23: *"From that time forth began Jesus to shew unto his disciples, how that he must go unto Jerusalem, and suffer many things of the elders and chief priests and scribes, and be killed, and be raised again the third day. Then Peter took him, and began to rebuke him, saying, be it far from thee, Lord: this shall not be unto thee. But he turned, and said unto Peter, get thee behind me, Satan: thou art an offence unto me: for thou savourest not the things that be of God, but those that be of men."*

Peter attempted to get Jesus to abandon his assignment of being killed. Peter said what most or all of us would say to a friend. Yet, Jesus rebuked him and called him Satan. Satan is known as the enemy. The rebuke although heard from the mouth of Jesus' friend Peter, the words were from the enemy Satan. Never assume that the enemy will always use the same approach.

Their tactics might be different, but the intent is the same. Reader, please take into consideration Judas.

"And forthwith he came to Jesus, and said, Hail, master; and kissed him. And Jesus said unto him, Friend, wherefore art thou come? Then came they, and laid hands on Jesus, and took him." (Matthew 26:49-50)

Jesus knew Judas had planned and executed his betrayal, yet Jesus called him a friend. Please understand that this is serious. Peter who was trying to have Jesus stay alive was rebuked but Judas who betrayed him was called a friend. I do not know about you but, Peter sounded more like a friend to Jesus than Judas. Therefore, do not fail to probe why Judas was called friend and Peter rebuked.

Based on scripture, from as early as Genesis 3:15, God declared that there would be enmity between Satan and the son of God (Jesus). Jesus came in the fullness of time and knew his assignment, his purpose. Although he meant well, Peter spoke against Jesus fulfilling his purpose. Jesus could not entertain any arguments intended to sway him from completing his assignment. Judas on the other hand, though he betrayed Jesus was acting more of a friend because he assisted him in completing his assignment. Some assignments will require the assistance of friends to be completed. Whether that assistance comes dressed as an ally or a foe, the result must be the evaluating rubric. Never be afraid to treasure an enemy who assisted in the completion of your assignment above a friend who sabotaged the same.

Based on this brief dialogue, we can cross over into this wealth; a friend helps you in fulfilling your assignment. This help sometimes can hurt, like Judas's. As was expounded in Mind Renewal: Biblical Secrets to A Better You, Judas was a destiny helper to Jesus. Judas was necessary to Jesus. Cross over into this painful but necessary truth - you needed the hurt.

Can I suggest to you that the person who hurt you, betrayed you, abandoned you, was an asset to you? You needed the rejection, to be fired, left, and divorced. It was good that you were sidelined and not given the promotion. The disappointments are designed to serve as your motivations. Have you been capitalizing on them? You cannot afford to waste your disappointments, hurts or pains; they are too valuable. In other words, they are your destiny helpers. Their assignment is to push you forward to birthing your destiny. Cross over with this intent; disappoint your disappointments. Your disappointments said you would go into self-pity, depression, withdrawal, etc.; but today, not tomorrow, take a stand and disappoint your disappointments.

Jesus collectively called his disciples friends but said one of them is a devil- Judas. Yet he approved his betrayal by calling him a friend. In other words, thank you Judas for helping me to fulfill my God given assignment. Are you willing to cross over in your minds to the place where you can thank your Judases? Thank that boss that fired you, ex that left you, the bank that did not approve your loan etc.

What about your pastor who overlooked you? Sometimes, the worst thing that could happen to you is an approval that was not sanctioned by God. Cross over into this light, purpose to reject every approval that was not sanctioned by God.

God approved Abraham to get a child by his wife and Sarah approved Abraham to get a child by Hagar. Two approvals but only one was of God. Please carefully consider this- whose approval are you living?

Peter disapproved of Jesus' declaration and was rebuked; Judas helped his declaration and was called a friend. It will not always look like it is in your favour, but if you look through the lenses of God, it will all make sense. Please look at approval through the account of Mary.

"Now the birth of Jesus Christ was on this wise: When as his mother Mary was espoused to Joseph before they came together, she was found with child of the Holy Ghost. Then Joseph her husband, being a just

147

man, and not willing to make her a public example, was minded to put her away privily." (Matthew 1:18-19)

Mary was approved by God but disapproved by the standards of men. Cross over into this truth, your approval is stamped at a level higher than the level of your disapproval. Earth disapproved but Heaven approved. Look at the words found in Jeremiah 1:4-5:

"Then the word of the LORD came unto me, saying, before I formed thee in the belly, I knew thee; and before thou camest forth out of the womb I sanctified thee, and I ordained thee a prophet unto the nations."

Your ordination was not dependent upon you. Your heavenly ordination comes despite your goodness and your flaws. Stop seeing negatives only from the lenses of pain. Reap the blessings from every negative encounter. Perhaps your partner has walked out of the marriage. That was painful but now you rejoice. Now you can truly say you appreciate that person who came into your union. You love him/her. That person is a friend who acted in a manner that caused you to be happy today.

Stop wasting precious resources on being angry, bitter, disappointed, or depressed. Thank God for the Judas who acted against you, rather than for you. They acted in your favour more than many friends would have. Can you not see this? Joseph helps you with the following words: *"But as for you, ye thought evil against me; but God meant it unto good, to bring to pass, as it is this day, to save much people alive."* (Genesis 50:20)

There resides your peace. Call your ex-partner, the person who broke your heart, the company that fired you, and tell them thank you. They acted better than a friend to you.

CROSS OVER KEYS

1. It is said if you have one good friend in a lifetime you are blessed.
2. Are you willing to cross over in your minds to the place where you can thank your Judases?
3. Purpose to reject every approval that was not sanctioned by God.
4. It will not always look like it is in your favour but if you look through the lenses of God, it will all make sense.
5. Your approval is stamped at a level higher than the level of your disapproval.
6. Never be afraid to treasure an enemy who assisted in the completion of your assignment above a friend who sabotaged same.

7. Your heavenly ordination comes despite your goodness and your flaws.

8. Reap the blessings from every negative encounter.

9. The disappointments are designed to serve as your motivations. Have you been capitalizing on them?

CHAPTER THIRTEEN

EVIL HELP

The word of God tells us in Psalms 121:1-2: *"I will lift up mine eyes unto the hills, from whence cometh my help? My help comes from the LORD, who made heaven and earth."*

The Psalmist asked the question, from whence cometh my help, and proceeded to answer his question with an absolute TRUTH– "My help comes from God."

The Psalmist is assuring that God will be the help he needs. At close examination, the passage is suggesting that not all help is from the God who made heaven and earth. Cross over into this truth, not all help is godly or good. Cross over in this wise, deceptive help is an agent of stagnation; premature help serves as a representative of abortion and wrong help is a silent assassinator. Let's examine these three types of help.

Deceptive help: One of the devices used by the kingdom of darkness is deception. We see this weapon as early as in Genesis. God told Adam and Eve not to eat of the forbidden tree and if they did, they will die. Satan told Eve she would not die. He told her, she would become wise, knowing good and evil. Satan gave the impression that he was helping her to discover herself at a higher level. The deception was disguised as help when in fact it was death. A need-to-know Cross over truth is this - not every help is the best available option accessible to a person, family, or nation. Every rendered help must first be evaluated based on the word of God before acceptance is pursued. This level of deception continues today but unfortunately is not recognized by many because it comes in the name of help.

In our modern society we are big on help. Helping is promoted as a means of assisting someone or a community that has fallen on hard times. One way of eradicating deception masquerading as help is by examining closely the ancient Chinese proverb which says, "Give a man a fish and you feed him for a day…. Teach a man to fish and you feed him for a lifetime." The hand-out system where a government or the rich gives to the poor in the name of help is a huge deception that continues to expand across geographical borders.

This system is designed to have the less fortunate continually be at the mercies of the society's privileged. This help system ensures that the poor never escapes the clutches of poverty and dependency. This type of help creates a ceiling which blocks the poor from expanding. However, if we are to terminate this deception, it will mean rather than giving a relief fish, you teach who would have been a recipient how to catch fish. Having received teaching, that person is now equipped to appreciate the necessary resources which would make fishing viable. This is called empowerment into independence and dignity.

Premature Help: The premature help is harder to identify but not impossible. We see an example hidden in the book of Genesis chapter 37: 21-22:

"And Reuben heard it, and he delivered him out of their hands; and said, Let us not kill him. And Reuben said unto them, Shed no blood, but cast him into this pit that is in the wilderness, and lay no hand upon him; that he might rid him out of their hands, to deliver him to his father again."

Rueben purposed to help his brother Joseph escape from the evil plans of his brothers. He divided his plan into two segments. The first which he succeeded at was preventing them from killing him; he saved his life. The second which he failed at was delivering him out of the pit and returned him to his father. What Rueben saw as failure was victory. If Rueben had achieved segment two, his premature help would have aborted Joseph's purpose and destiny. The dreams that Joseph had dreamt resided behind the curtains of betrayal from his brothers. Rueben meant well but failed to see what God was allowing to unfold was the door to a bigger picture. The purpose for the betrayal, and the failed premature help was made known in chapter 45:4-8 which reads:

"And he said, I am Joseph your brother, whom ye sold into Egypt. Now therefore be not grieved, nor angry with yourselves, that ye sold me hither: for God did send me before you to preserve life. For these two years hath the famine been in the land: and yet there are five years, in the which there shall neither be earing nor harvest. And God sent me before you to preserve you a posterity in the earth, and to save your lives by a great deliverance. So now it was not you that sent me hither, but God".

Look carefully at what Rueben's well-meaning premature help would have aborted - their future. God used their betrayal to preserve their future.

A dear friend of mine went through a series of closed doors; every seemingly possible assistance dried up. During that time another friend who is always willing to assist, was also going through a rough patch and was unable to help. We crossed over to this truth that God made it tight so that help could not be rendered. Bail out helps which would seem like the best thing a friend could do to another, would have been the worst option. It would have released on her, wrapped in that gift, the cruelty of stagnation. That help would have dwarfed her growth and prevented her from ever knowing God at the level He was taking her. The indelible truth is that significant growth is achieved on the backs of adversary. Adverse situations can easily be your best friend. Cross-over into this truth; to reject all pre-mature help is good futuristic investment.

Wrong help: In a class of twenty students, John was among those who were struggling to grasp the subject's concepts. John resorted to asking his friend for assistance who unreservedly did the work for him. At the end of the semester, John sat in the course final exam and panicked. He did not know the material and could not answer the questions; he failed the course which meant he could not take up the one-time football scholarship offer that awaited him. John was silently assassinated by wrong help.

The help was sought by him, but he blundered in the acceptance of the easy way. The easy way was his friend doing it for him. The hard and necessary route was his friend teaching him the concepts. Just like the easy way is giving a man a fish while the hard and needed path is teaching him how to fish. The help he accepted willingly was his demise. Like John, if you fail to reject the easy way for the hard and needed, the result will be you reaping the un-pleasantries hidden in deception. He was deceived into believing that he was being helped. In 2 Samuel 13, we see an account of wrong help which led to deception, rape, and murder. Ammon the son of King David loved his half-sister, Tamar, and became sick because of how he felt towards her. His cousin asked him what caused him to be troubled and he told him of his love. He submitted the following advice recorder in 2 Samuel 13:5:

"And Jonadab said unto him, Lay thee down on thy bed, and make thyself sick: and when thy father cometh to see thee, say unto him, I pray thee, let my sister Tamar come, and give me meat, and dress the meat in my sight, that I may see it, and eat it at her hand."

Tamar went to dress meat for Amnon, and he raped her. Absalom, her brother, learned of this crime against Tamar and after two years killed Ammon. Ammon received wrong help in the form of strategy to get Tamar in his house. This help eventually led to his death. Cross over in this wise, any help that is not godly has poisonous venom secretly hidden and will be released at an appointed time. Evaluate every help offered against the standards or word of God.

CROSS OVER KEYS

1. Not all help is godly or good.
2. Deceptive help is an agent of stagnation; premature help serves as a representative of abortion and wrong help is a silent assassinator.

3. Every rendered help must first be evaluated based on the standard of the Word of God before acceptance is pursued.

4. The indelible truth is that significant growth is achieved on the backs of adversary.

5. Adverse situations can easily be your best friend.

6. To reject all pre-mature help is good futuristic investment.

7. Any help that is not godly has poisonous venom secretly hidden and will be released at an appointed time.

CHAPTER FOURTEEN
THE EAGLE IN YOU

International motivational speaker Les Brown shared the following story from which I purpose to extract some powerful cross over truths. He said a farmer found an eagle's egg one day and placed it among the chickens. After a few days, the egg hatched, and the eaglet was born. The eagle grew and was nurtured as a chicken. It scratched and picked worms from the ground. One day an eagle glided above, and it caught the attention of the eagle on the ground. The eagle on the ground enquired about the magnificent bird above. A chicken told him, that is an eagle. He is the king of the air, but we will never be like him, we are only chickens. The eagle on the ground was born an eagle but lived and died as a chicken. According to Isaiah 40:31: *"But they that wait upon the Lord shall renew their strength; they shall mount up with wings as eagle."*

This tells us that an eagle is strong and powerful. Yet in the above account, the eagle's strength was never known because of its culture. Journey with me as I extract as promised, some powerful truths from the eagles' story.

1. You do not have control over the circumstances that precedes your birth. You were not consulted with

regards to the country of birth nor the family in which you were born. Therefore, your beginning was decided by your parents. The egg must have fallen from the nest but for whatever reason, it was not retrieved. Many persons today battle with questions concerning their origin. Some were abandoned at a hospital, with grandparents or even at a church. Others have never seen their father, as he left after being told his girlfriend was pregnant. Cross over into this light; the hand you have been shared is not the conclusion of your life. You must take charge and evolve from the broken to the best.

2. The eagle was a victim of its environment. The familiar place dictated the values and worth ascribed to self. Eagles are known to have excellent eyesight, but its vision was blurred by the surroundings in which it was born and lived. Nurture crushed nature. The same is the truth for many persons today. The environment of nurture has dictated very low dimensions of habitation. The possibilities to rise have been blocked. The truth is there are persons who are so grateful for the assistance at low level; they refuse to think outside of that realm. Cross over into this powerful truth; misappropriated gratitude is a barrier to expansion. Never allow your appreciation for past good done, to prevent you from

increasing to new levels of gratitude. There are differing levels of gratitude. Be conscious that attaining appreciation at level seven does not mean you ceased being grateful at level three.

3. This might be challenging to embrace but cross over into this truth; there is more available than what has been offered. The day you exhaust that which has been made available to you, is a strong indication you have outgrown your space. The choice is yours, you can either develop a workable cycle of adjustment to the existing norm or you can pursue more. This is where you chose to exist or live. Let the excellent difference in others inspire you to rise to greater.

4. Even though the eaglet was raised as a chicken, it observed magnificence. It saw the eagle and was attracted to the beautiful gliding across the skies. Please do not ignore the inner pull you receive when you are graced with excellence. Let this pull motivate you to seek knowledge. Do not be afraid to ask the hard questions. For the eagle one question he could have asked is, why do I look so different? Please be conscious that it is a futuristic crime to not pursue one question with other questions. The conversation the eaglet had with the

chicken should never have ended where it did. Cross over in this light, ask questions.

5. The chicken said to the eagle, we are only chickens. Please never allow anyone to dictate your maximum. You might be in the same space, family, and rank but their conclusion of themselves, does not have to be your summary. It is up to you to embrace your current state or cross over.

To avoid being added to the statistics of those who lived and died without ever knowing who they were, you must have a serious mental cross over, mind relocation from the grounds of chickens to the mountains of eagle. You will never pursue what your mind has not envisioned. To discover and live who you are, will require you to dig deep. The rubbles of (chicken-ness) have buried you so deep, it will require intentional pursuit to escape. Cross over into this light; you do not have to die not knowing your God given identity.

Look at what happens when you are living a failed life. The discussion that took place was between two possibilities- a predator and a prey, eagle, and chicken. The eagle is an enemy of chickens, but the defeated eagle is seen here receiving schooling from a lower bird. No matter your beginning, it is time to arise to your rightful place.

Here is a controversial truth with a twist. The eagle was raised as a chicken and thus its strengths were never realized and utilized. If the chicken had been raised as an eagle its weaknesses would still retain. E.g., it will still be unable to soar as an eagle. The worst-case scenario, the chicken that thinks it is an eagle will be eaten by the others.

Lesson: An eagle raised as a chicken still has the potential to be an eagle, but a chicken raised as an eagle will always be a chicken. If you are a chicken, be the best chicken. But if you are an eagle, which I believe you are, never settle at the place of chickens. The eagle in you needs to find that place of release; release the greatness in you that you have been relinquishing all your life.

CROSS OVER KEYS

1. The hand you have been shared is not the conclusion of your life.
2. The environment of nurture has dictated very low dimensions of habitation.
3. Misappropriated gratitude is a barrier to expansion.
4. Never allow your appreciation for past good done, to prevent you from increasing to new levels of gratitude.
5. There is more available than what has been offered.
6. Let the excellent difference in others inspire you to rise to greater.

7. Please do not ignore the inner pull you receive when you are graced with excellence.

8. You will never pursue what your mind has not envisioned.

9. Please do not ignore the inner pull you receive when you are graced with excellence.

10. Please never allow anyone to dictate your maximum.

11. You will never pursue what your mind has not envisioned.

CHAPTER FIFTEEN
FAITH

It is imperative to study the word of God. In it you will find life. As you study the word of God, please understand that Bible study is supposed to challenge you to become a better you. To become better will require alterations to the present. No one can promise you that life will be all easy. However, let the tight places in life usher you into a closer relationship with God. Whenever you go into studying the word of God and you are challenged, do not run away. Rather run into the scripture some more.

According to Hebrews 11:1, *"Now faith is the substance of things hoped for, the evidence of things not seen."*

The hope that you need are the spiritual lenses of God. This permits you to see beyond the natural availabilities of our senses - things seen through the physical lenses. Cross over in this wise, faith is the perspective from which you must receive and accept your dictates or instructions from. Let the eyes of faith be your personal constant navigation system. Faith is so powerful it challenges you to trust that which is not within human comprehension. Recently I was told of a Christian businessman who heard in the spirit, to withdraw all his money from a trading company. He obeyed and called his broker with instructions to do withdrawal immediately. Ten minutes later, the broker called back asking how he knew. The broker said, ten minutes after he called, the company went under. His perspective of the company changed as he got spiritual navigation which he received and accepted by faith. Faith and obedience saved him millions and years of sacrifice. Will you allow faith to work for you?

Faith sees where the physical eyes are prevented because of limitations. Faith sees beyond barriers, graves, sickness, setbacks, disappointments. Faith takes you places years before your physical feet can tread there. Please embrace this cross over truth, where you fail to walk in faith; you will never walk in sight. My mother had nerve issues that negatively affected her sleeping desires. One day she was listening to Oral Roberts on the radio, and he said, "You are having issues with your nerves, lay your hand on the radio cabinet and believe by faith and receive your healing." She did and received her healing instantly. She believed and received by faith.

Faith is not just hoping; it is a currency. Cross over into this light; what you can obtain by faith is more than what the currency called money can buy. Apostle Joshua Selman said, if money is the only currency you employ, you are poor. Faith is the currency of counteraction against what is opposing your today. It is your faith that is going to make you unstoppable in this season. It is your faith that will cause you to break barriers and receive what God has given you. It is your faith in God that will cause you to be obedient to Him and receive from Him. Begin to think in faith, speak in faith, then act in faith and finally, receive in faith. Walk in the currency of faith.

Faith functions as a Master Key. It is not restricted to any area or subject. It has unlimited access to truth and righteousness.

Matthew 8:5, *"And when Jesus was entered into Capernaum, there came unto him a centurion, beseeching him, And saying, Lord, my servant lieth at home sick of the palsy, grievously tormented. And Jesus saith unto him, I will come and heal him. The centurion answered and said, Lord, I am not worthy that thou shouldest come under my roof: but speak the word only, and my servant shall be healed. For I am a man under authority, having soldiers under me: and I say to this man, Go, and he goeth; and to another, Come, and he cometh; and to my servant, Do this, and he doeth it. When Jesus heard it, he marveled, and said to them that followed, Verily I say unto you, I have not found so great faith, no, not in Israel. And Jesus said unto the centurion, Go thy way; and as thou hast believed, so be it done unto thee. And his servant was healed in the selfsame hour."*

Abide in this truth, Jesus can be marveled. Faith demonstrated captured the marveling component of Jesus; this is nothing ordinary. When you think about who Jesus is, -the Creator of all things, it is extraordinary that He was marveled by the man's faith. It is time for you to marvel heaven.

The centurion understood not just authority, but words. Do you understand words? A person who understands words, is slow to speak and quick to listen. Look closer to what happened. Jesus was not where the centurion's servant was, yet he understood that the spoken word of the anointed Jesus knows where to locate his servant. Faith's Navigational system was activated. For too long your activation button has been untouched, it is time to press the activation button, this is achieved through faith and believe in Jesus.

The released word through faith is not just a navigational system, but also a game changer. Faith is a verb which means an action word. Cross over in this wise, your faith must be demonstrated by your matching actions. One young lady shared that she saw an ad, she holds a bachelor's degree, but the job required a master's degree. She heard in her spirit, apply. She did not meet the requirements, but the Holy Spirit said, "Apply." By faith she obeyed and applied God honored her faith and gave her the job; she is still working in the position.

Remember faith is a master key. It opens doors you are not qualified to venture into. Faith goes where intellect (qualifications) cannot take you. Education is excellent and should be pursued but not at the expense of faith. The activated faith takes you to horizons that you have no point of reference. You become the point of reference. In the book of Genesis, Noah had no ark to refer to. He had never seen or heard of any Ark being built. But by faith he built an Ark and became the point of reference for generations.

Recently someone speaking about her Christian experience said, "Today, there must be more than this." And I agree. There is more. The more that will never be found without moving from your present place to faith. Faith is that vehicle that moves you from the average to the more - the more that is available. A dear friend of mine was moved from the average by faith and obedience; she was instructed to resign her job' which sounds crazy. A single mother, with rent to pay and two sons to care for, quitting her job? She was told by the Holy Spirit to focus on ministry. Truth is, it has been rough, but God has not failed her. Cross over in this wise, faith will never take you beyond the capabilities of God.

Another young lady got an opportunity to go overseas to work. She gave her husband the opportunity and she stayed with the children. He went, returned, and went again, then never came back. He abandoned her, divorced her, and remarried. She said, the Lord told her, he is her husband. He will bring them back together. It has been 13 years now and she is still waiting. Faith is not only a master key or a vehicle, but also a source of sustainability. Many men have come her way, but she believes and is waiting in faith. Faith makes waiting be without weight. As she waits upon the Lord, her strength is renewed daily.

For too long you have accepted so much good, you have no room for the best. We are cornered by sight which says, 'hog say the first water you get, wash'. But faith says, 'I will wait for God's best'.

God's best for you is not necessarily the new job, the marriage or excellent working hours etc. His best is you having faith in Him. He said without faith you cannot please Him. Please assess how we have been operating. Are you living based on sight or faith?

Most times you hear about faith giving, we think the preacher is talking about money. Well maybe you are correct. But this faith giving is you giving you. Give you until it messes up your plans. Do you give within the safe zone of your peace? In other words, does your giving disturb your comfort? Sight giving does not ruffle any feathers but faith giving messes up plans, routines, and logics. Faith cannot be wrapped in intellect or reasoning. Please carefully ponder this question; can God trust you to give Him you in complete faith?

I was working on a project and needed much help. A dear friend decided to help me. When she saw the huge task, she said, "can I just give money?" Answer was no. The giving that was required was not money; that is easy giving; however, when you give yourself that is a different level of giving.

We ignorantly do not appreciate or understand faith giving of self because of the emphasis placed on money.

There are two different levels of faith giving. 1-putting a gift on the altar versus 2-you being on the altar. Cross over into this truth; faith giving is committing yourself to that which is uncertain to you but certain to God. We see faith giving in the early account of Abram.

Genesis 12:1, *"Now the LORD had said unto Abram, Get thee out of thy country, and from thy kindred, and from thy father's house, unto a land that I will shew thee"*

The faith that was required was him giving himself and submitting to God's instructions. We are exhorted in scripture to give unto the Lord, let us look at Deuteronomy 14:22: *"Thou shalt truly tithe all the increase of thy seed that the field bringeth forth year by year."*

Tithe is prescribed as ten percent but that is average. Pay attention to Hannah in the book of 1 Samuel 1:11: *"And she vowed a vow, and said, O LORD of hosts, if thou wilt indeed look on the affliction of thine handmaid, and remember me, and not forget thine handmaid, but wilt give unto thine handmaid a man child, then I will give him unto the LORD all the days of his life, and there shall no razor come upon his head."*

Hannah made a faith covenant with God. She spoke about giving her son to him while she was still at a place of barrenness. That is a high-level covenant. Her physical conditions said barren, but her faith said produce. Cross over with this; if all you can see is within the limitations of your physical eyes you are deprived. She made good on her promise and gave Samuel to the priest. Hannah gave not tithing of a tenth - she gave all (Samuel).

The once barren Hannah, by faith gave all she had before and after her womb was opened. Then looked what happened. *"And the LORD visited Hannah, so that she conceived, and bare three sons and two daughters. And the child Samuel grew before the LORD."* (1 Samuel 2:21)

This is the level of Faith we need to pursue. The word pursue means follow or chase (someone or something). Synonyms: go after, run after, follow, chase, and give chase to.

This dimension of faith will not be achieved by an accident or from being casual. It is speaking about being intentional in faith. Remember that faith is a currency of trade. It's like the barter system. The degree of your investment determines the magnitude of your returns. It is like this - give sparingly, reap sparingly, give bountifully, reap bountifully.

In the economy of heaven, operations function on the premise of addition and multiplication. One seed sowed in faith has the potential and capabilities to give a cycle of perpetual lifetime returns. There are rewards you are benefiting from now, that you did not sow, but your forefathers did. You are entrusted with NOW, to secure the future by faith for your children and the generations to come. This is true; remember Solomon fought no war because his father King David, through his many victories, secured a peaceful reign for his son. What are you by faith, securing for your children?

Heaven's Economy is operated by laws of integrity. Integrity law: #1. When you sow in good soil you must reap. Notice, it was not just when you sow; but the soil is important. Jesus gave a parable, in Mathew 13 where He spoke about four different soils. Only one was good. Hear this hard truth, you say you are sowing into a person's life and ministry etc., but you did not do a soil evaluation. Cross over with this powerful truth; not all soil is good.

I see an evil parading in the churches. Your local pastors are in need. They are the ones who have been toiling with you, but you never sowed a seed into their life. But a foreign speaker comes, and you sow rent, tithe, and your children back to school monies. You know nothing about the speaker (the soil), but you sowed. In the economy of heaven, the citizens are owned by the King. Everything you possess is owned by the King. That includes your time, money, ears.... whatever you use as a seed. Therefore, you must get directions from the owner. You cannot do whatever you choose with what does not belong to you. The day you accepted Jesus, you gave up ownership as you were bought by His blood/life.

Sorry to be the one to tell you this - God does not need your money. Whenever God requires something from you, it is because He wants to increase you. But, because the kingdom is governed by principles and laws, He gets you involved.

Your main barrier to wealth and prosperity is your failure to have faith in God, which comes from lack of knowledge. How is this? Remember faith is a master key. If you do not activate the key, doors remain closed to you.

I remember a minister was asked to pray with someone. He did and the person was blessed. The person in gratitude wanted to bless the minister financially. But he responded, "That is ok." Now is not the time for you to give to me, this is my time to sow into your life. What the person did not know was the minister needed the money. However, he was not released to accept. Faith in God will help you to be offered what you need but cannot accept because Heaven said no. Now this can be tight, but when you understand that heaven is not broke, you can trust heaven. If an agent on earth wishes to bless you and heaven says do not accept, Heaven knows why. Please look at some possible reasons:

1. The soil it is coming from is contaminated. Some gifts are poisonous. It is better to be in lack than to be filled with poison. Please be conscious of this truth; poison does not always bare the label poison.

2. What was offered was not what God told the person to give. That offering represented you being robbed. If you accepted it, you would have been agreeing with being robbed. It would not end there. It would have been the commencement of a series of robberies against you. Here

is an example. God spoke to John saying, bless Mary with twenty thousand dollars ($20,000). John disobeyed and gave Mary ten thousand dollars ($10,000). Mary was so in need, she rejoiced and blessed John's hands, his business, and his family. She blessed the robber.

3. God is testing your love and obedience for and in Him against the desires to see your lack being fulfilled. Do you love the provisions more than the provider?

4. The person who was instructed to give was being tested. Like Abraham sacrificing Isaac. Your obedience to God in rejecting the gift helped to complete the test.

5. The anointing. There are persons who sow into the demonstrated anointing and not the person. Without the anointing, they would never stretch a hand to you. Therefore, you must be careful of what you invite to partake of the anointing. Years ago, the Lord said to me, the anointing is not for sale. Therefore, if you see where someone is trying to buy into your anointing, that seed must be rejected. We see a perfect example in the book of Acts 8:18-21: *"And when Simon saw that, through laying on of the apostles' hands, the Holy Ghost was given, he offered them money, saying, give me also this power, that on whomsoever I lay hands, he may receive the Holy Ghost. But Peter said unto him, thy money perish with thee, because*

thou hast thought that the gift of God may be purchased with money. Thou hast neither part nor lot in this matter: for thy heart is not right in the sight of God."

Please hear this – do not be fooled by the followers of the anointing. They are not your ride and die. They are not your friends; they are trying to be friends with the anointing, not you. You are liked by default because you are the carrier. They want what they did not get through faith. It is an attempt to trick heaven. Cross over into this light, faith is the protocol. Remember, without faith it is impossible to please God.

CROSS OVER KEYS

1. Faith is the perspective you must receive and accept your dictates or instructions from.
2. Faith is so powerful it challenges you to trust that which is not within human comprehension.
3. Faith sees where the physical eyes are prevented because of limitations.
4. Where you fail to walk in faith, you will never walk in sight.
5. Faith is the currency of counteraction against what is opposing your today.
6. Faith functions as a Master Key.

7. Your faith must be demonstrated by your matching actions.

8. Faith will never take you beyond the capabilities of God.

9. Faith is not only a master key or a vehicle, but also a source of sustainability.

10. Faith makes waiting be without weight.

11. Sight giving does not ruffle any feathers but faith giving messes up plans, routines, and logics.

12. Faith giving is committing yourself to that which is uncertain to you but certain to God.

13. If all you can see is within the limitations of your physical eyes you are deprived.

14. This dimension of faith will not be achieved by an accident or from being casual.

15. Faith in God will help you to be offered what you need but cannot accept because Heaven said no.

CHAPTER SIXTEEN
TIGHT PLACES

Tight places are opportunities for growth and to see the miraculous. As you encounter the tight places, be adamant that nothing will stop you from serving your God.

In 2019 I did a series teaching on 'the tight place'. One day as I taught, I had to rush my daughter to the hospital. I sat in the emergency room and taught on the tight place. The devil told me my daughter was going to die. But I pushed that aside and pushed to do God's will. My daughter recovered and is still doing great at home. The tight places require faith and confidence. Submitting to God in a tight place can be difficult but very rewarding.

The Lord took me through a period where everything failed/crashed. At the point where lack of food was my house's friend, I could not pay utilities, nor could I afford to go to church. In that tight place the Holy Spirit said, start a prayer meeting and Bible study in the living room and invite the people of the community.

This request from God was unbelievable. How could He ask me to do this at a time when I could not feed my family? I had to take the children out of private school and sell the vehicles.

178

I was unable to purchase basic necessities like tissue and toothpaste. How could He tell me to invite persons into my home, who were in a better position than I am? After I pour out and is hungry, they go home to their big dinner?

Cross over in this scary yet powerful truth, if you are submitting to God only in your place of abundance and peace, you have not truly learned submission. Jesus taught one of the most powerful acts of submission when he cried to His Father in the Garden of Gethsemane. In Luke 22:42, Jesus said, Father this is heavy, this is a tight place, nevertheless, not my will but thine be done. (Submission in a tight place). God trusted Jesus with this tight place. Can He trust you with tight places? Submission in a tight place is not talking about feel good, or good conditions serving, but when everything you have is required.

As I submitted to the Holy Spirit In that tight place, I saw persons of not good societal standard, and others who outside of the directives of God, I would not invite into my home, sitting in my living room, listening the word of God, and being prayed for. I do not know what the Lord has been telling you to do - it is rough and tight, but hear me, you need to submit.

My ex-wife and I had a falling out and I was kicked out of the house. I had nowhere to sleep, and a friend got somewhere for me. As I lay there on the bed, I asked God, 'why am I at this house?' He responded, "you are here to support the host". This was a tight place, but ministry was required of me. Despite my own pain, I was called upon by God to attend to the pain of another. Jonah found himself in a tight place, and he repented and submitted. Let us look at Jonah 2:1-9: *"Then Jonah prayed unto the LORD his God out of the fish's belly, and said, I cried by reason of mine affliction unto the Lord, and he heard me; out of the belly of hell cried I, and thou heardest my voice. For thou hadst cast me into the deep, in the midst of the seas; and the floods compassed me about: all thy billows and thy waves passed over me. Then I said, I am cast out of thy sight; yet I will look again toward thy holy temple. The waters compassed me about, even to the soul: the depth closed me round about, the weeds were wrapped about my head. I went down to the bottoms of the mountains; the earth with her bars was about me forever: yet hast thou brought up my life from corruption, O LORD my God. When my soul fainted within me, I remembered the LORD: and my prayer came in unto thee, into thine holy temple. They that observe lying vanities forsake their own mercy. But I will sacrifice unto thee with the voice of thanksgiving; I will pay that that I have vowed. Salvation is of the LORD."*

Notice in vs 9, he said, I will pay that which I have vowed, submission. After he repented and submitted, look what happened in Jonah 2:10: *"And the LORD spake unto the fish, and it vomited out Jonah upon the dry land."*

His repentance and submission activated the voice of God. God spoke concerning him. God desires to speak in the matter that concerns you, please allow Him to. God spoke to a fish/whale, and it obeyed. There are some non-speaking elements that are going to cooperate with God in this season with regards to you. You have been expecting God to use humans but be it known, God is not limited. What you do not see spelled out in the text is, the fish/whale getting instruction as to the direction to go. As soon as the Lord spoke to the fish/whale, he was spat out at his place of assignment. This tells you the direction was given.

There are some non-speaking elements that have been given directions as to your location or where you are going to be. They will find you!

Will you submit to God in difficult circumstances such as when your spouse is cheating, you lost a loved one, got fired from a job, lost all your monies, did not get the visa, the guy you are dating suddenly married someone else, your marriage is failing, your business crashed, or you had a car accident?

Jonah was literally in a tight space (cannot get any tighter than in a fish's belly). How tight is your space? Your space is extremely tight, you feel like you cannot even breathe. Yet your answer must still be, yes, I will submit. Submission in the tight place is a recipe for an explosive miracle.

Jonah wanted to see more than 120,000 persons punished. He preached but did not want the people to receive the message and repent. How do you handle the tight place where you want judgement; you want revenge, but God says restoration? God sent Jonah to Nineveh, a people who were enemies to Israel. If God desires, He will send you to those who have hurt you.

Look how tight it was for Jonah. Jonah 4:2-3: *"And he prayed unto the LORD, and said, I pray thee, O LORD, was not this my saying, when I was yet in my country? Therefore, I fled before unto Tarshish: for I knew that thou art a gracious God, and merciful, slow to anger, and of great kindness, and repentest thee of the evil. Therefore now, O LORD, take, I beseech thee, my life from me; for it is better for me to die than to live."*

Jonah thought it better for him to die. That is a serious heart condition. Why would God use someone who had such a severe heart condition? He repented in the fish's belly but look at his response now. Was his repentance genuine or was it out of fear? Where is your repentance from? Do not miss this, He preached, and the entire city repented, yet his heart was not right.

A great cross over truth is, great reception to your ministry does not mean you are in right standing with God. The reception means God did what he purposed to do.

One wife was being abused by her husband for going to church. He used the watering hose to wet her down on Sundays as she left for church. However, she went to church in the wet clothes. It caused the husband to suspect she had a man at church, so he decided to trail her. He followed her straight to church. He watched his wife. She was in love with God. That same day he surrendered his heart to God. Cross over to this truth, your submission to God creates an opening for someone to receive life changing transformation. Your submission is powerful.

My mentor Rev. David Grant was invited to minister at a church. That weekend, he had no monies for his four children to go back to school on Monday. When he got the invite, he blessed God because maybe, he might get a love offering. Reader, he got the love offering and God said, sow it back into the ministry. This is a place you need to cross over into-nothing you have is better than submission to God. He obeyed and gave back the needed money to the church. He submitted but it was not easy. Please embrace this truth - if submission was easy, it would not be a place to be renewed into.

David having submitted in a tight place received far more than what he sowed. It is a principle. You do not sow one and reap one. Cross over to this knowledge-Whenever God instructs you to sow, please understand, He wants to bless you abundantly. All He is doing is getting you to submit and partner with Him. God never requires more from you than He is prepared to give to you. The tight place is not designed to kill you, but to bless you. I rejoice with everyone who is in a tight place now. Only submit to God and you will be ushered into the abundance.

In Genesis 21: 8-21 we see the account of Sarah telling Abraham to put his son Ishmael out of the house. Abraham loved his son Ishmael, yet God told him to submit to his wife and put him out of the house. There are some situations that are tight and smooth others are tight and rough. This indeed was a tight and rough place. For eighty-five (85) years he was childless, then he got Ishmael and God told him to put him out. What is it that is within your house or your life that you love dearly, but God is saying, put it out? I besiege you to submit and put it out.

A young lady I studied with at the Victory Bible Institute said, in seeking the Lord, she was told by God that He will be sending her on mission trips and on one of the trips, she is going to die. Since then, she was led to study nursing and is presently working as a nurse. She made her first oversees ministry assignment last year. Look how God is setting the stage. Missionary as a nurse- she submitted. Is the Holy Spirit speaking to you? Will you submit to God in the tight/rough places?

In 2013 the Lord spoke to me, He said I should leave my homeland, He is sending me to a land I knew not. After I cleared some outstanding debts, I managed to leave Jamaica with $25 USD. I landed and stayed with a pastor. I applied for a job and was told I was successful. However, I did not start until six months later. During that time, I had no monies to send back to my wife and children, who were all in school. I was not asked to, but I volunteered myself to be the house helper. I needed to be contributing where I was eating and sleeping. I cooked, cleaned, etc. My mother called one day, and said, Leo the Guidance Counseling job you applied for back here in Jamaica, has been approved. You need to come back home, take the job, and provide for your family. I said to her, I am sorry but that is not what the Lord is saying to me. He is not telling me to return. I am going to trust Him to work it out. This is the truth, it was not easy, it was tight, but God worked it out. Cross over in this wise, the easier choice might not be the will of God. Was I being a bad father and husband? To some it would appear that way, but I knew I was submitting to the will of God in a tight place. Today we are all living together again.

I will end this segment by sharing a scenario for your consideration:

A Christian girl gets raped and finds out she contracted a sexually transmitted disease. Now after doing a dilation and curettage (D&C), three months later, going through the ordeal of the rape, she now finds out she is pregnant. As a Christian, should she abort this child? This child, who will be a daily reminder of her being raped. Will she be able to love and connect with the child? Should she bring the child and give it up for adoption? This indeed is a tight rough place. Truth is, some might say do an abortion although that child might be the only child she may ever have. This young lady maybe feeling angry, frustrated, and upset with God, as well as other tummy-aching emotions.

Submission is a process. God intentionally allows or puts you in tight spaces for His purpose. If flesh keeps operating, then you will not be able to experience God's greater glory. Some spaces are extremely tight that at times they make it hard to breath. But when Jonah was in His tight space that is when he cried out to the Lord.

I wish you would not get these life's packages, enabling you to glide through life effortlessly, but you cannot. However, please cross over in this wise, the greater and tighter the spaces, the greater the divine revelations. Cross over into your cross over.

CROSS OVER KEYS

1. Submitting to God in a tight place can be difficult but very rewarding.

2. If you are submitting to God only in your place of abundance and peace, you have not truly learned submission.

3. Submission in the tight place is a recipe for an explosive miracle.

4. Great reception to your ministry does not mean you are in right standing with God.

5. Your submission to God creates an opening for someone to receive life changing transformation.

6. Whenever, God instructs you to sow, please understand, He wants to bless you abundantly.

7. Submission is a process. God intentionally allows or puts us in tight spaces for His purpose.

8. The greater and tighter the spaces, the greater the divine revelations.

About the author

Jamaican born, Rev. Leostone Peron Morrison, is the author of the book, Mind Renewal: Biblical Secrets to a Better You and the three-part Mind Renewal Devotional Series among other books. He has served as an Assistant Pastor and Guidance Counselor at the Ministry of Education in Jamaica. He served as Probation Officer in the federation of Saint Kitts and Nevis. Rev. Morrison is the founder of Restoration of the Breach without Borders Ministry, of which, Restoration of the Breach School, hosted on the Thinkific platform, is a subsidiary. He is the founder of Next Level Let's Climb Bible Study Ministry. Bathroom cleaning was his first ministry assignment.

He is a graduate of the Jamaica Theological Seminary and holds a Bachelor's Degree in Theology, with a minor in Guidance and Counseling. He acquired a diploma in Biblical Principles from

Victory Bible School, and a certificate from the International Accelerated Missions School (IAMS). Rev. Morrison is married and has four sons and one daughter.

NOTE: For feedback, consultation or speaking engagements contact Rev. Morrison at restorativeauthor@gmail.com. Kindly submit a review on Amazon or the platform where you bought this book. Thank you.

Other books by the author

Mind Renewal: Biblical
Secrets to A
Better You

Mind Renewal Transformational
Devotional Vol. 1

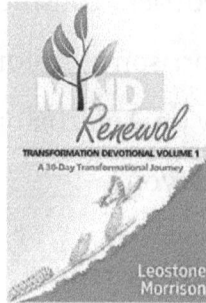

Mind Renewal
Transformational
Devotion Vol 2

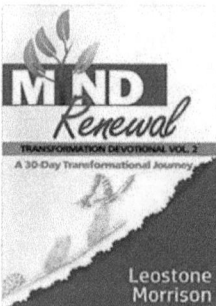

Mind Renewal
Transformational
Devotional Vol 3

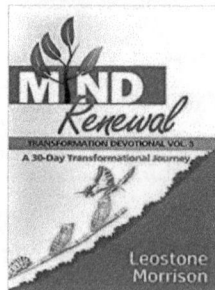

Marriage Reconstruction
Where Victories and Errors Teach

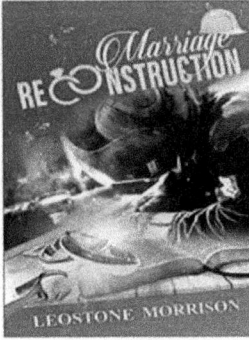

Pray Through
The Book of Psalms: 150
Days

Marital Intimacy

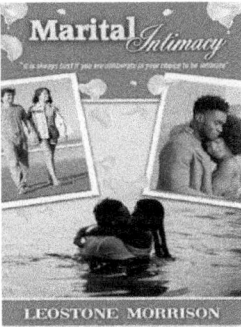

Bishop Judas: Powerful Hidden
Lessons

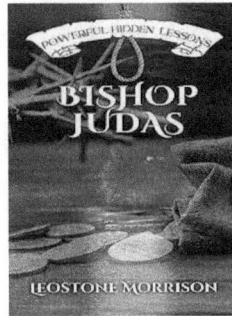

Boot Camp Workbook Journal:
A Spiritual Journey

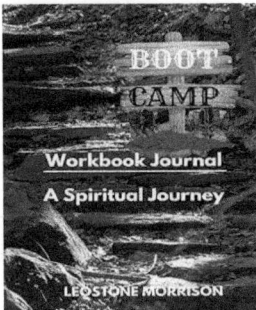